RUUSBROEC AND HIS MYSTICISM

Paul Verdeyen, S.J.

translated by André Lefevere

A Michael Glazier Book

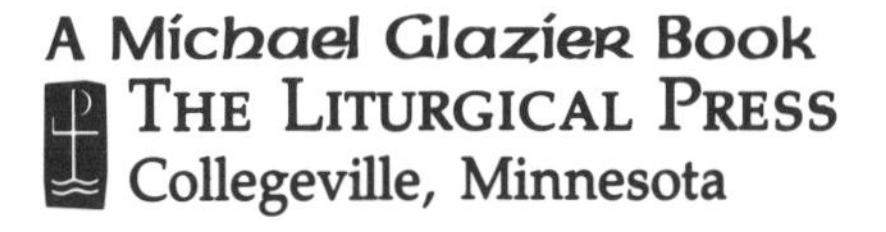

A Michael Glazier Book published by The Liturgical Press

Cover design by Don Bruno
Woodcut by Robert McGovern

The publisher is grateful to the University of Antwerp for permission to reproduce the portrait of Ruusbroec and the Praeconiale of Groenendaal, both belonging to the Ruusbroecgenootschap.

1 2 3 4 5 6 7 8 9

Library of Congress Cataloging-in-Publication Data

Verdeyen, Paul.
[Ruusbroec en zijn mystiek. English]
Ruusbroec and his mysticism / Paul Verdeyen ; translated by André Lefevere.
p. cm. — (Way of the Christian mystics ; v. 11)
"A Michael Glazier book."
Includes bibliographical references.
ISBN 0-8146-5628-5
1. Ruusbroec, Jan van, 1293–1381. 2. Mystics—Belgium—Biography.
I. Ruusbroec, Jan van, 1293–1381. Selections. English. 1994.
II. Title. III. Series.
BV5095.J3V4213 1994
248.2'2'092—dc20
[B] 93-47034
CIP

Contents

I. RUUSBROEC'S LIFE (1293–1381)

1. The Sources 9
2. Study in Brussels (1304–1317) 12
3. Chaplain of Saint Goedele (1317–1343) 15
4. Which Heretics Did Ruusbroec Attack? 19
5. A Survey of the Works Written in Brussels 24
6. The Founding of the Monastery at Groenendaal (1343) 31
7. Transition to a Religious State (1350) 41
8. Ruusbroec in the Groenendaal Community 45
9. How and Where Ruusbroec Wrote His Later Works .. 47
10. Groenendaal Writings for a Brussels Poor Clare 49
11. The Origin of the Last Works 55
12. The Brothers of Groenendaal 64
13. Ruusbroec and the Carthusians 69
14. Visitors at Groenendaal 72
15. Ruusbroec and Geert Groote 75
16. Last Years 79
17. Veneration and Beatification 83
18. The Circulation of Ruusbroec's Works 86
19. Gerson's Criticism of the "Espousals" 90
20. Ruusbroec's Influence on Later Writers 92

II. ANTHOLOGY

1. The Work of God in Man 99
2. The Three Stages of Spiritual Life 102
3. A Hymn to Holy Trinity 110
4. What the Senses Experience During the Encounter with God 112

5. The Ideal of the Common Life 115
6. Encountering God in Christ 118
7. Chapters on the Eucharist 123
8. Ruusbroec as an Exegete of Holy Scripture 128
9. The Mystic's Symbolic Language 136
10. A Sober View of People and Situations 142

Conclusions 159

Quotable Sayings 162

Bibliography 164

The Old Ruusbroec Portrait

The portrait was painted on heavy paper, glued to a small wooden panel and framed by a small old black frame. The portrait itself measures 64 by 93 mm. It is reproduced here according to its real size. The small painting has been at the Ruusbroecgenootschap since 1924. It was given to L. Reypens S.J. by the reverend Bernard, dean of Maasmechelen. Before that it had belonged to Monsignor Bogaerts, vicar-general of the bishopric of Liège. The Reverend Bernard himself wrote down the story of how he received the painting.

> In 1840 Monsignor Bogaerts was sub-regent at the Pope's College in Leuven. During that time he wrote some articles on medieval preachers, among them Ruusbroec. One day, after the Ruusbroec article had been published, Monsignor Bogaerts found the portrait on his desk. He later learned that it was a present given by the Reverend Michiel Davids, then curate at Louvain and later priest of Drogenbos near Ruisbroek. Monsignor Bogaerts kept the portrait as a valuable memento. He spent the last years of his life (1882 to 1891) at Zonhoven, where I was chaplain then. I was his confessor and I had to administer the last rites to him. After his death his inheritor allowed me to select a memento. I chose the portrait and it has remained in my possession since.

The portrait's artistic merit has been well described by father L. Taeymans S.J. in 1924. "Around 1550 the painter of the portrait copied a probably much older miniature. He omitted some parts of the original. It would appear that Joannes Ruusbroec is sitting in front of a table, and that he lets his left hand rest on the arm of a chair, while the right hand—the movement can be inferred from the folds in the sleeve—rises in a gesture of blessing or, rather, writing." The sixteenth century painter managed to keep the typical face of his model and the inspired look in the eyes very well. Because of this, father Reypens looked for the possible painter among the Windesheim chapter miniaturists. He suggested the name of Aegidius van der Hecken, canon of Zevenborren, who died in 1538.

In father Taeymans' opinion this portrait is based on an older model. It is not too bold to suppose that this model was painted at Groenendaal. This brings L. Reypens to the hypothesis that the oldest Ruusbroec portrait was painted at Groenendaal by Jan Spieghel van Cureghem, one of the good prior's brethren from 1351 to 1358, and that Ruusbroec actually sat for the portrait himself. Jan Spieghel van Cureghem was a remarkably good painter and illustrator of manuscripts. He died at twenty-four and Willen Jordaens wrote a remarkable funeral elegy about him. But the portrait's older model has been lost and hypotheses of this kind lack all foundation in fact.

I

Ruusbroec's Life (1293–1381)

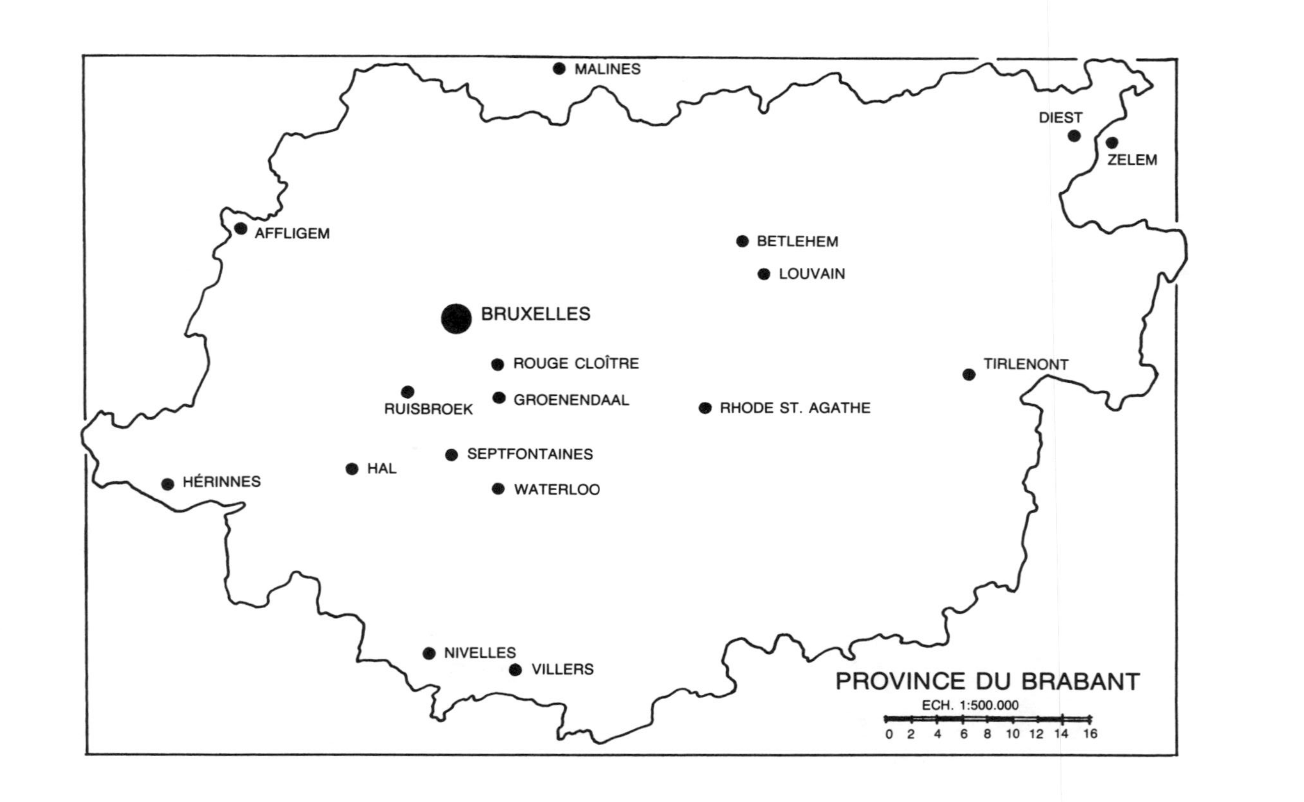
MALINES
DIEST
ZELEM
AFFLIGEM
BETLEHEM
LOUVAIN
BRUXELLES
ROUGE CLOÎTRE
TIRLENONT
RUISBROEK
GROENENDAAL
RHODE ST. AGATHE
SEPTFONTAINES
HAL
HÉRINNES
WATERLOO
NIVELLES
VILLERS
PROVINCE DU BRABANT
ECH. 1:500.000
0 2 4 6 8 10 12 14 16

1

The Sources

Ruusbroec's teachings are much better known to us than his life. Eleven treatises and seven letters describe exhaustively the many aspects of his spiritual teaching. But his life escapes historical investigation for the most part. His works have always found quiet readers and admirers. Zealous copiers often copied them on parchment or on paper: more than two hundred manuscripts bear witness to their work. But for Ruusbroec's life we have to make do with a biography containing many data that turn out to be unreliable, three testimonies by contemporaries, and incidental information gathered from the painstaking study of archives scattered all over.

The only book on Ruusbroec's life was written around 1420, in Latin, by the Augustinian canon Hendrik Utenbogaerde, better known under his Latin name Henricus Pomerius (+ 1469). It was not his intention to write down an accurate historical report, but rather to tell a devotional story about the first prior of Groenendaal. That story follows the stereotypical pattern of the medieval lives of saints. That is why the exemplary man of God has to be holy from the first days of his life onward; he has to abandon his possessions as soon as possible, hold worldly wisdom in contempt, and both recognize and frustrate all snares set for him by the Evil One. It is not easy to separate fact from fiction in that type of text. Pomerius did not know Ruusbroec personally, and he wrote his book forty years after Ruusbroec's death. He therefore had to rely on written or oral data he could get from older brothers. He names two of them by name in his prologue: Jan van Hoeilaart (+ 1432) and Jan van Schoonhoven (+ 1431). Especially the latter seems to have contributed much material, because we read in the obituarium (the list of deceased brothers) of Groenendaal that this "Johannes de Scoenhovia" had himself written a life of Ruusbroec, in which he gave an eyewitness account. Unfortunately this older biography did not survive and that is why Pomerius's story set the pattern for all subsequent historiography. Pomerius's Latin text has been preserved in fifteen manuscripts, and it had already been translated into Dutch in the fifteenth century. In fact Pomerius wrote a threefold memoir in which he summarized the history of the foundation of Groenendaal, and of its first inhabitants. The first part is entitled *The Origins of the Groenendaal Monastery* and it is followed by the biographies of Jan van Ruusbroec and Jan van Leeuwen.

It is hardly surprising that Pomerius devoted most of his attention to the mystic's later years, when Ruusbroec gave the new community its own proper stamp in his capacity of prior and spiritual leader. He had little precise information at his disposal about Ruusbroec's youth and education. Ruusbroec's stay in Brussels and his activities as a young priest remain vague. He must have belonged to the clergy of St. Goedele cathedral, but we do not know what his function was. Could he have been the chaplain of one of the guilds' chapels or had he entered the service of some rich canon as that canon's substitute (vicarius)? In what surroundings did he carry out his apostolate? What contacts did he have with the Brussels beguines and with the followers of the Free Spirit? Pomerius has very little to say about all this and his scant data are often contradicted by other sources.

The three contemporaries and eyewitnesses of Ruusbroec's life also have little to impart about his youth, his education, and his stay in Brussels. But their contribution is very important for the Groenendaal period. The main direct witness is Jan van Leeuwen (+ 1378). He joined the Groenendaal community as early as 1344 and made himself useful as the monastery's "good cook" until the time of his death. Ruusbroec himself taught him to read and write, and he was also his confessor and spiritual guide. The good cook wrote no less than twenty-three treatises about the spiritual life and in them we read a few moving eulogies on his "unforgettable and glorious confessor, my lord Jan van Ruusbroec, prior of Groenendaal."

A second contemporary is the founder of the Devotio Moderna, Geert Groote (1340–1384). He himself visited with Ruusbroec at

Groenendaal. He wrote him a letter and mentioned him several times with high praise in other items of his correspondence. The third eyewitness is brother Geraert, the Carthusian monk Geraert of Saintes, who received Ruusbroec around 1360 in the Carthusian monastery of Herne. This monk had planned to copy several of Ruusbroec's works in a single manuscript, to preserve them for his monastery in that way. He introduced that manuscript with a prologue he wrote himself, in which he talks about the visit Ruusbroec paid the Carthusians of Herne at their own invitation. In this way brother Geraert provides us with the only account of Ruusbroec's life that did not originate in the sphere of the Groenendaal monastery or in the circles of the Modern Devotion. The historical importance of this prologue has to be strongly emphasized, also because of its content.

2

Study in Brussels (1304–1317)

Jan van Ruusbroec was born in 1293 in Ruisbroek, a village in the valley of the Zenne, nine kilometers south of Brussels. We know very little about his family. They were probably not without means, because later in life Ruusbroec was to transfer his right of inheritance to the Groenendaal monastery. That right of inheritance amounted to "six and a half pounds and ten capons" a year. A rich priest, chaplain of St. Goedele in Brussels, was a member of his family. This uncle, Jan Hinckaert, gave his nephew a fixed annuity of eight pounds in 1327, or one eighth of the profits of a windmill in Schaarbeek, together with a dividend *in natura,* to be collected off a plot of land in Ganshoren. Ruusbroec's father is not mentioned in any source. His mother is, more than once. According to Pomerius, little Jan escaped from his mother's tender care at the age of eleven to go live with his uncle in Brussels. The uncle generously accepted the boy into his household and sent him to the cathedral school where he was given the opportunity to learn Latin and to be educated in "grammatica, retorica, and dialectica." According to Pomerius, Ruusbroec attended school in Brussels for only four years. After that, he bade farewell to all human knowledge, following the example of Saint Benedict, to search only for divine wisdom with all his power and zeal. This information provided by the biographer should probably not be taken too literally: everything written at Groenendaal was written with the avowed intention of especially emphasizing Ruusbroec's direct contact with God himself. The good prior's writings and his spiritual teaching were considered a direct gift from the Holy Spirit by his contemporaries. For that same reason Pomerius underestimates the importance of the education

Ruusbroec was given in his youth. The influence of his social and cultural milieu is also neglected. "This man of God was blessed with the dew of the Holy Spirit to such an extent, and he was given such deep spiritual insight, that he not only transcended the labyrinth of human logic, but also the difficult exertions of philosophy and the high speculations of theology."

Ruusbroec's writing did indeed originate in a special inspiration, but there is no reason to assume that the divine inspiration could not have worked together with human culture and endeavor. When he was about sixteen the young student had gone through the three subjects constituting the *trivium* in the Saint Goedele chapter school. He could now further pursue his studies at the university of Paris or at the famous school of Cologne. Young and intelligent people from Brabant tended to study in both locations during the fourteenth century. Yet it seems most improbable that Ruusbroec enjoyed this kind of higher education. The data at our disposal do not completely exclude that possibility, but they certainly do not point in that direction. Ruusbroec obviously did not receive a university degree. On that level he was definitely of lesser stature in Groenendaal. Moreover, he was either a chaplain or a substitute priest in Brussels for twenty-five years. It is almost inconceivable that a priest with a university education would have been allowed to carry out these humble tasks for so long.

Without a university education Ruusbroec persevered in studying on his own. The well-known writer Maurice Maeterlinck definitely goes too far when he states that Ruusbroec "did not know Greek, and probably not even Latin." Ruusbroec's works prove very obviously that his knowledge went beyond the first principles of the Latin language. He translated long chapters from Latin books into his own mother tongue. He read difficult and erudite texts in Latin, understood their contents very well and took over their concepts in his own spiritual teaching. We also know that the young chaplain was ordained priest when he was twenty four-years old. Even in the Middle Ages candidates for the priesthood were supposed to know more than young altarboys.

Where did Ruusbroec acquire the necessary knowledge, and how? Our knowledge of both the organization of the Brussels chapter school and its curriculum is sadly limited. In 1179 the third Lateran council ordered all chapter schools to pay for a magister who was to teach their own clergy. We are entitled to suppose that attempts were made in Brussels, too, to lift the young cleric's knowledge of the Bible to an acceptable level. Priests were not just supposed to say Mass, they also had to sing the daily office in a sensible manner and to preach the Word of God at suitable times. Hence they had to know the sense and the meaning of the main truths of the Christian faith. Ruusbroec himself later wrote a short commentary on the twelve articles of the creed, known to us under the title: *The Christian Faith*. He must have received similar instruction before his ordination as a priest. It is not very probable that only his uncle would have taken care of his ecclesiastical training. But we do not know how the young cleric was really trained.

Ruusbroec's mother is explicitly mentioned in Pomerius's description of the young chaplain's ordination. She herself had moved to Brussels about 1305, and she had gone to live in the local beguinage "to enjoy the nearness of her son at intervals more frequent than would have been possible in the country." It was not given to her to witness his actual ordination in 1317. Ruusbroec later told his brethren that she would often appear to him in a dream with the question: "My dear son, how much longer will it be before I see you standing at the altar?" On the day when he offered his first Mass to God, the young priest received a divine sign that his mother had been admitted to heavenly joy. She appeared to him again to testify that his first Mass had delivered her from the pains of purgatory.

3

Chaplain of Saint Goedele (1317–1343)

Brother Geraert of Herne wrote down one sentence only about the first part of Ruusbroec's life: "My lord Jan van Ruusbroec was first a pious priest and chaplain at Brussels in Brabant, in the Church of Saint Goedele, and there he began to make some of these books." A most concise summary of a period of twenty-five years, and yet the Carthusian monk mentions the only fact we know with any certainty about Ruusbroec's stay in the capital of the Duchy of Brabant: that he was a simple chaplain who began to write mystical treatises. Indeed, his first five treatises were all written in Brussels itself. Before his departure for Groenendaal Ruusbroec also wrote the first part of his longest treatise: *The Spiritual Tabernacle.* Ruusbroec experienced peaks of mystical revelation while working as a simple priest in a busy urban environment. His spiritual life is no sweet fruit of the quiet and remote Zoniën forest South of Brussels; it had its roots in the bustle of city life and came to full fruition in the same environment.

Why did Ruusbroec begin to write down his spiritual experiences? Probably to achieve clarity for himself, in the first place. His first book, *The Realm of Lovers,* was not written for a particular audience, because Ruusbroec regrets the fact that the copier had given it to other readers without letting him know. Religious texts in the language of the people were obviously in high demand. Brother Geraert writes: "At that time there was great need of spiritual reading matter in the language of the people, especially because hypocrites and groups professing false doctrines attracted attention. Ruusbroec clearly described those people at the end of the second part of *The Spiritual Espousals* and he often refers to them elsewhere in his books."

For what audience did Ruusbroec write his works? Some texts were written in answer to requests made by specific persons. Ruusbroec wrote for an anonymous hermit in the Zoniën forest, for Poor Clares in Brussels and for the Carthusians of Herne. He also wrote *against* specific people, but without mentioning them by name. Brother Geraert writes about "hypocrites and groups professing false doctrines." Pomerius supplied this vague reference with a name and a face in his story of the Brussels beguine Bloemardinne.

Pomerius' reading of history has become the subject of incisive historical research since the beginning of the twentieth century. It has to be admitted that this research does not only not confirm his reading of the facts in any way; it contradicts them clearly. Yet it seems appropriate to relate this story from the years of Ruusbroec's stay in Brussels in Pomerius's version first.

> There lived in Brussels, in the years when Ruusbroec was a secular priest there, a heretical woman, named "Bloemardinne" by the people. She was held in such high esteem that she was accompanied by two seraphs when she went up to the altar for communion, they say. She wrote much about the movement of the *Free Spirit* and about sinful love and lust, calling the latter "seraphic." Since she founded a new doctrine she was deeply revered by her many followers. When she taught or wrote she sat on a silver chair and that chair was later offered as a relic to the Duchess of Brabant. Handicapped people mobbed her deceased body in the hope of finding healing and salvation. Our man of God, full of the Holy Spirit, was very disturbed by this erroneous doctrine and opposed this perverse heresy from the very beginning. Even though he met with much opposition, he clearly unmasked the aberrations and heresies she spread for years by means of her supposedly inspired writings, in total opposition to the true faith. In that way Ruusbroec obviously proved to what extent he was filled with the Spirit of strength and wisdom, because he did not fear the snares of his enemies at all and he was not for a moment misled by the beautiful exterior of false arguments written down under the guise of truth. I can testify from my own experience that her execrable writings exhibit such an obvious semblance of truth at first reading

> that nobody can suspect a germ of error in them, except with the Holy Spirit's special grace and assistance.

A number of elements taken from this story can be compared to other historical sources. The duchess of Brabant was probably Maria of Evreux, a woman of great piety with outspoken mystical leanings, who died in 1335. Bloemardinne herself is no stranger to history either. The name Heilwigis Bloemaerts, called Bloemardinne, appears repeatedly in the official documents of the Brussels aldermen between 1305 and 1336. Many bills attest to the fact that she took great pains and spent much money to found a retirement home for older women. Ruusbroec's uncle, Jan Hinckaert, even appears as a witness on the last deed Heilwig Bloemaerts had drawn up on July 6, 1335, in which she declares she owes one hundred pounds to a certain Cornelis van Ninove. All these data seem to corroborate the fact that Pomerius's Bloemardinne did indeed live in Brussels and that Ruusbroec must have known her relatively well. Heilwig Bloemaerts was a beguine in the original meaning of the word: a pious and socially conscious woman who led a normal civic life. She founded a retirement home and acted as its director, which brought her high esteem among the people.

Pomerius's data therefore appear to be wholly truthful in as much as he describes the life and social situation of this well-to-do and generous lady. We may conclude from the aldermen's documents that she died around 1335. It is remarkable that Ruusbroec never attacked her in any personal manner: he only unmasks the errors and the heresies that can be found in her writings. Yet Pomerius immediately calls this benefactress a heretical woman, *mulier perversi dogmatis.* This opinion is seriously questioned by historical research.

Was Heilwig Bloemardinne really a heretic? There are sound arguments to contradict this opinion of Pomerius's. Not only did not a single text written by this woman survive, we also find no evidence anywhere that such texts even existed. Moreover, nothing is to be found in history about any heretical movement in Brussels in the first half of the fourteenth century. It is known, on the other hand, that a procession of flagellants moved through the Low Countries in 1349. These brethren, who whipped themselves in public as a way of doing penance, may also have attracted attention in Brussels. Nothing is known about this with any certainty and Ruusbroec nowhere mentions the movement. There is also a more positive reason to doubt Bloemardinne's heretical influence. Her works of charity and her foundation for poor older women survived her. The direction of the retirement home is taken over by the chapter of Saint Goedele in 1371 and its founder is remembered with great respect in the deed of transfer. She is described in it as a "laudabilis persona et in Christo devota": a person deserving of much praise and linked to Christ in devotion. In addition to this, the clergy of Saint Goedele commemorated her Christian death until the beginning of the sixteenth century. These data are hard to reconcile with Pomerius's reading: if this generous woman had spread a nefarious doctrine the Brussels church would not have been able to celebrate her pious memory without calling forth opposition. We may therefore conclude that Pomerius unjustly describes this Brussels beguine as the "right-minded Ruusbroec's" heretical counterpart.

4

Which Heretics Did Ruusbroec Attack?

No matter how improbable Pomerius's Bloemardinne story, the fact remains that Ruusbroec described and attacked certain forms of extra-ecclesiastical mysticism (which he considered heretical) in his works. Nowhere did he mention these opponents and false prophets by name. Yet the mystic, normally so mild, has very severe words for them: "They live in opposition to God and all the saints: they resemble the spirits of the damned in hell." Which concrete persons or which spiritual movements is Ruusbroec thinking of? It is risky to suggest an answer here because the problem has not yet been studied in sufficient depth. But even a hypothesis can help in answering certain questions. Let us therefore turn to a passage from *The Spiritual Espousals,* a text Ruusbroec wrote in Brussels before 1343.

> These people opt for a purely passive subjection, without any activity directed toward God or their fellow men, because they think they would hamper God in his work if they performed even the slightest work themselves. Hence they remain devoid of all virtues to the extent that they do not want to either praise or thank God, that they possess neither knowledge nor love, and that they themselves no longer want, pray, or desire. For whatever they might be able to beg for or desire they already possess, in their opinion. They are so poor in spirit that they are without will, that they have abandoned everything, and that they live without self or any preference. They think they already possess all things the exercises of Holy Church serve to attain and for which they were instituted. It is hard to recognize these people unless you yourself are illuminated (by the Holy Spirit)

> because they are often ingenious and able to hide their aberrations under flowery language, or else they write commentaries to explain them. They are so selfrighteous that they would rather die than change their opinion on any point (CC-CM 103, pp. 552–560).

The warning against ingenious reasoning and aberrations concealed underneath flowery language can also be found in Pomerius, and it is clear that he took the concept from Ruusbroec's text. But in which text was Ruusbroec himself able to read the objectionable theses he so sharply condemns? Which text propagates relinquishing all virtues, the total obliteration of one's own will and intellect, the rejection of all desire because one is convinced one already possesses everything? All these theses are to be read in a still too little known treatise entitled *The Mirror of Simple Souls.* The original French version of this treatise was published by Romana Guarnieri in 1965. This same scholar also proved convincingly that the book was written by Margaretha Porete, a well-known beguine from Valenciennes, a city that belonged to the Low Countries until 1677.

Until recently the name of Margaretha Porete was known to us only from the acts of the French Inquisition. This pious, courageous, and probably utterly orthodox beguine was burnt at the stake in Paris on June 1, 1310, on account of her so-called heretical writings. It is apparent from well-kept archives that Margaretha Porete was called to account by bishop Guy of Cambrai before 1306. This bishop condemned her book as heretical and had it burnt in public in Valenciennes in her own presence. In addition, Margaretha had to promise that she would no longer give such writings to others to read. Her book had probably already been circulated on too large a scale for all traces of it to be erased. It attracted attention again in 1310 in connection with an examination ordered by the inquisitor William of Paris and conducted by twenty theologians of the University of Paris. The inquisitor showed the suspect book to the learned gentlemen, but he only allowed them to read two theses he had taken from the book. These theses brought the assembled theologians to the unanimous conclusion that the text was not orthodox and deviated from the true faith. The verdict of the Paris professors led to Margaretha's condemnation as a relapsed heretic, and eventually to the stake. The two theses that led to the condemnation can indeed be found in the Latin text of the treatise, *Speculum simplicium animarum.* When lifted from the context of the totality of the book they sound like the stupid affirmations of a muddled mind. The first thesis holds that certain souls no longer need to apply themselves to the Christian virtues: "The soul lost in love bids the virtues farewell and stands no longer in their service; it no longer has to apply itself to the cultivation of the virtues; rather, the virtues themselves are at its service" (CC-CM 69, p. 29). The second thesis deals with God's gifts of grace: "This soul is no longer concerned with God's comfort and his gifts; it does not need to concern itself with them any more, indeed it cannot do so, because it has directed its attention completely to God himself" (CC-CM 69, pp. 93–95). The two theses quoted here can almost literally be read in Ruusbroec's text quoted above, in which he described some misguided people. These people assert that they can do without all virtues and that they no longer have to beg for anything, or desire anything because they already possess everything since God himself is enough for them in all things. Such people are convinced that they have completely lost their own will, that they need neither knowledge nor love, and that they no longer have to worship God with praise and gratitude.

The writings of the Brabant mystic lead us to suspect that he was strongly impressed by Margaretha's testimony. He never omits the importance of human effort and growth in all kinds of virtues. He calls this active way "active turning inward." But this active way can be followed only in the light and warmth of divine love. Otherwise one only believes in salvation through works. Those who bask in the divine sun are trained in "essential turning inward." Both aspects of that one human experience have been described with the pen of genius in the following passage from *The Spiritual Espousals:*

> As soon as God observes any capacity in us to receive his grace, He wants to bring us to life out of his free goodness and He wants us to resemble Him by means of His gifts. This happens whenever we turn ourselves totally towards Him with our will. For at that same moment Christ comes to us and in us, *mediated and unmediated,* that is: with His gifts and beyond all gifts. And we also come to Him and in Him, mediated and unmediated, that is: with virtues and beyond all virtues (CC-CM 103, p. 478).

This union, mediated and unmediated; God's influence through His gifts and through His direct nearness; our turning inward through the virtues and beyond them: these three main concepts are to be found just as clearly in *The Mirror of Simple Souls* as in *The Spiritual Espousals.* Margaretha discusses them in a passionate and provocative tone; Ruusbroec does not have that direct and personal tone, but his formulation is crystal clear and exceptionally precise.

It seems fairly certain that Ruusbroec himself knew and read the *Speculum simplicium animarum.* Did he also know the author's name? We cannot infer anything from the fact that he does not mention her anywhere. Did Ruusbroec consider the author and her work dangerous and heretical? Nothing is less certain if one notices the relationship between their teachings. Why, then, his outspoken rejection? Why does he write so aggressively against certain theses that are found in Margaretha's *Mirror?*

This last question can only be answered by referring to the consequences of Margaretha's work and her dramatic death for the life of the Church in the fourteenth century. The beguine movement found it very hard to gain acceptance by the Church's hierarchy. In 1215 the fourth Lateran council had forbidden the foundation of new mendicant orders. The second Lyon council reinforced this prohibition in 1274. In 1312 the council of Vienne condemned certain aberrations particularly espoused and propagated by some beguines. The sixth condemned thesis reads as follows: "To cultivate deeds of virtue is necessary for imperfect people; the perfect soul bids virtues farewell." This allows us to conclude that certain isolated opinions of Margaretha Porete had gained currency among the beguines as quotes out of context. The personal testimony of Margaretha's *Mirror* had been twisted by anonymous readers and admirers and distorted in muddled theological and moral theses.

Everything points to the fact that Ruusbroec must have known certain people in the Brussels beguinage he regarded as victims of a relatively widespread mystical movement. These people considered themselves spiritually perfect, having attained the highest degree of contemplation, or vision of God. Not only did they hold all external activity in contempt, they also rejected all authority exerted by the official Church and all possible criticism from learned theologians. Later historiography called them followers or friends of the *Free Spirit.* Ruusbroec understood immediately the threat this movement represented to the development of a healthy spirituality within the Church. He did not call on the inquisition: his faith in the efficiency of external power and repression was too limited for that. But in his many writings he tried to divide chaff from wheat as honestly as he could.

Close-up of Ruusbroec walking around town

When Jan van Ruusbroec was still living in the world as a priest he devoted so little attention to his outward appearance that he seemed like a poor fellow to all those who only knew him from a distance. He was a quiet man of few words, poorly dressed, but civilized in conversation. He walked through the streets of the city as a hermit would have. He did not venture outside often because the serenity of contemplative prayer agreed much more with him than external activities. It happened once that he was walking through the streets of Brussels, completely absorbed in his mind by heavenly thoughts. When two burghers observed him walking past and noticed his simple exterior, one said to the other: "If only I were as holy as that priest walking past there." But his companion replied: "I wouldn't want to be in his situation for all the gold in the world, for what pleasure would I have left then?"

Ruusbroec, who happened to hear those words, replied silently by himself: "How little you can even suspect the sweetness people enjoy who are allowed to taste the Spirit of God" (Pomerius, De vita et miraculis fratris Johannis Ruusbroec, in: *Analecta Bollandiana* IV, 1885, pp. 285–286).

5

A Survey of the Works Written in Brussels

1. The first book Ruusbroec wrote was given the title *The Realm of Lovers.* The Carthusian monk Surius was to clarify this title later in his Latin translation and call the work *Regnum amantium Deum,* i.e. *The Realm of the God-loving Souls.* Ruusbroec wrote his first work long before his departure for Groenendaal, probably between 1330 and 1340. Later, when Ruusbroec visited the Carthusians at Herne, he was surprised that they owned this book. He told them he was sorry the book had become known and that it had been circulated. It had been passed on to the Carthusians in secret by a priest who had been Ruusbroec's notarius (or clerk). When the Carthusians wanted to return their text to him he did not want to accept it. He probably knew the text had become known elsewhere, too. He promised them he would write another book to explain the difficult sections and to make his meaning clear. He did so in his last work, *The Little Book of Enlightenment.*

The Realm of the God-loving Souls describes the spiritual life as a steady progress towards God through the workings of the Holy Spirit in His seven gifts. The Herne Carthusians had great difficulties with Ruusbroec's description of the gift of *counsel.* In fact, Ruusbroec does not stick to the pattern of steady growth and progress. Under the gift of counsel he discusses the necessary interaction between prayer and action, practical virtues and the being with God in joy. These two poles of the spiritual life are also connected with Life in God himself. The sublime Trinity is admired by Ruusbroec, both in the quietude of Its essential unity and in the works of the three Persons. In this description Ruusbroec resembles a boiling kettle of water, says Pomerius, unable to hold in the fire of his experience, but forced to let everything steam out at once. Later he will be able to better schematize his experiences and to order them, although he always remains conscious of the fact that no description can ever completely express the direct experience.

2. The Brabant mystic's most structured book is undoubtedly *The Spiritual Espousals.* It has been called his masterpiece, and rightly so. Apparently, it immediately made a great impression on all those who got to know it. Brother Geraert talked about it with Ruusbroec himself.

"Of his second book, *The Adornment of the Spiritual Espousals,* he said he considered it a sure and good work and that it was already being copied, even at the foot of the mountains." The Carthusian's information is corroborated by a note written in Strassbourg by Rulmann Merswin (+ 1382):

> I want to describe a fruitful and useful teaching I found in the first part of a book about the (Spiritual) Espousals. It was written by a good and holy secular priest from Brabant, called "Johannes Rüsebruck" and he sent it to the friends of God in the "Oberlant" in the jubilee year 1350.

Ruusbroec's Dutch text was translated into Latin before 1360 by the Groenendaal brother Willem Jordaens (+ 1372). The translator wrote a remarkable letter of dedication in Latin to the Cistercians of the abbey Ter Doest who had asked for such a translation. The monks of Ter Doest thought the differences between Ruusbroec's Brabant dialect and their own West-Flemish dialect were too great to allow them to completely enjoy and assimilate the work in its original text. Geert Grote also translated this treatise of Ruusbroec's into Latin and he must have recommended it to many people. Yet he is the first to mention some theological reservations in connection with Ruusbroec's teaching, as early as 1383. The German theologian Henricus van Langenstein (+ 1397) asserted that *The Spiritual Espousals* contained many errors. Hence Geert Grote proposed that Ruusbroec's brethren in Groenendaal should change certain words that had to be rejected in their literal meaning. But he did not doubt that the good prior's meaning and intention had been completely sound and healthy.

How did Ruusbroec achieve the solid literary structure that makes this treatise into a masterpiece? He presents the whole treatise as a commentary on one sentence taken from the gospel of Matthew: "Look, the Bridegroom comes, go out to meet him" (Matthew 25:6). The sentence is taken from Jesus's parable of the wise and foolish virgins. The entire development of the spiritual life, of man's growth to a personal encounter with God, is tied to this quote. Ruusbroec distinguishes three stages in this growth that have become classics in all manuals of spirituality: the active life, the interior life, and the life spent in the contemplation of God. First, he exhaustively described the soul's moral growth as the result of the efforts involved in the active life. The second stage he calls the interior life, or the life spent in desiring God. "Interior" in this context does not just mean "turned inward," but also "simplified and concentrated in the depths of the heart." On this level man discovers that his own efforts are by no means sufficient to find God. He has to leave the rudder to the divine helmsman who will want to chart the course himself from now on. This implies that man's faculties abandon their own travels at that moment and embark on a voyage with an unknown destination. Ruusbroec is very precise in establishing the difference between moral life and the life spent in desiring God. In the first life, man tries to collect virtues in order to beautify his own house. People who devote themselves too exclusively to these works of perfection become slaves of their own efforts to achieve salvation through works. They will devote more attention to their service than to Him they serve. In the interior life, attention is concentrated exclusively on Christ's advent in man's soul. This second part of the *Espousals* can be seen as a deeply elaborate spiritual communion in which man becomes truly conscious of God's presence in the ground of his spirit. Such spiritual communion implies a conscious and direct encounter between man and his Creator. This spiritual encounter is the fundamental concept of *The Spiritual Espousals.* It has been beautifully expressed in the next passage:

> In this storm of love two spirits fight against each other, God's Spirit and our spirit. God bends himself into our inner being through the Holy Ghost and we are touched there in love. And our spirit penetrates into God through God's action and our loving power, and bends itself into his inner being, and God is touched by it. The fight of love originates from these two

> movements: every spirit is wounded by love in this deepest encounter and innermost and most penetrating visitation.
>
> These two spirits, our spirit and the Spirit of God shine on and illuminate each other and each shows the other its face. This makes the spirits long for each other in a similar fashion. Each spirit demands of the other all that it is and each spirit offers the other all that it is and invites it to partake of it. This makes the lovers flow into each other. God's touch and His gifts, our loving, longing, and giving in return keeps the love alive. This flowing out and flowing back cause the fountain of love to overflow. And so God's touch and our love's longing become one simple love. Man is possessed by love so much that he has to forget himself and God and know of nothing save love (CC-CM 103, p. 464).

In the third part, Ruusbroec deals with the perfect contemplative life spent in the vision of God. Ruusbroec was well aware of the fact that only a few on earth achieve such a high and intimate union with the divine mystery.

> Few people are able to achieve such a divine contemplation because of their own incapacity and because of the hidden nature of the light in which one contemplates. And that is why nobody will be able to understand the meaning of this vision of God in every detail by means of instruction or by his own profound reflection alone. For all words remain far below the reality I mean. But those who are united with God and instructed by Him are able to understand this truth (CC-CM 103, p. 576).

3. The third book written in Brussels is called *The Sparkling Stone.* Brother Geraert describes it as follows: "It should be known about this book that my lord Jan once sat talking with a hermit about spiritual matters. As they were about to say their farewells, the brother implored him to write down the conversation for further elucidation, so that he himself and somebody else, too, might be able to read it and progress in the life spiritual. And at this request he made this book, which in itself alone contains sufficient teaching to lead a man to a perfect life." This description is corroborated by a short dialogue to be found in the middle of the work. An unknown listener suddenly asks the writer: "But now I would like to know how we can become hidden sons of

God and possess the contemplative life." Ruusbroec's answer to this question contains a number of sentences in the second person, so that this work may be considered a report of an oral conversation. In matters of content *The Sparkling Stone* is very close to the *Espousals*. It contains at the same time a summary and an elucidation of what Ruusbroec wrote in his masterpiece. Hence this short work is the most accessible to today's reader. In the first part the reader finds the description of four categories of good believers: the hired hand, the faithful servant, the trusted friend and the hidden son. Even though all these believers strive to avoid evil and cultivate virtue, each in their own manner, they live the same Christian faith in very different ways. St. Paul speaks in his letters of children who still need milk and adults who are able to digest solid food. It is understood, of course, that the child will achieve adulthood under normal circumstances. This normal growth and development is lacking in Ruusbroec's description: there is no obligatory progression from hired hand to servant, from friend to son. What we are reading is a description of the free gifts of God awarded to some elect individuals for the benefit of the whole. It is clear that Ruusbroec intended to describe the mystic's own function and meaning within the totality of the Christian community. *The Sparkling Stone* was translated into Latin at Groenendaal by Willem Jordaens.

4. The fourth work is called *The Four Temptations*. It was translated into Latin by a Norbertine monk from Park (probably Simon van Wevel). This short treatise describes four temptations that can lead beginners in the spiritual life astray. Ruusbroec is not writing for people who are openly living in great sin, but for all those who want to live their faith in depth. The four main temptations are: life according to the lusts of the body and the senses, a hypocritical behavior inspired by too much penance, arrogant confidence in one's own erudition, and escape into laziness and false emptiness.

5. Ruusbroec's fifth book is called *The Christian Faith*. It is a short explanation of the twelve articles of the creed. It is the simplest work Ruusbroec has written, probably the result of his own catechetical work and his own instruction in the Brussels cathedral. Only the teaching about the life eternal is elaborated in a lively description of heaven and hell. The legend or exemplum

of the three gluttonous monks illustrates the more popular style of this teaching.

> Once upon a time there were three monks there by the Rhine who always went to eat outside the monastery. Two of them died suddenly and unexpectedly. One was strangled and the other drowned while bathing. Then one of the dead came back and appeared to the third companion, who was still alive. He told him that he was damned. Then the monk who was still alive asked him if his pain was severe. The other monk lifted his hand and let a drop of sweat fall on a tin or bronze candlestick that happened to stand there. And it melted in one second as if it was wax in a glowing oven. And the stench became so bad that the monks had to evacuate their monastery for three days. And the monk who saw this left the monastery and became a Franciscan. And the man who told me the story had also been a monk there and he had become a Dominican (CC-CM 110, pp. 428–430).

6. Ruusbroec's longest work, *The Spiritual Tabernacle,* was also written mainly in Brussels. This treatise contains an elaborate and free commentary on the building of the ark of the covenant as described in the Old Testament (Exod 26 ff.). The Jewish services in the temple and the different kinds of sacrifices are discussed in detail. The many biblical references become as many symbols for the spiritual ascent of the soul. This symbolic explanation of the Scriptures is less interested in the first and literal meaning of the text. Hence Ruusbroec's modus operandi is somewhat strange for today's reader. But this text was avidly read and held in high esteem during Ruusbroec's life and well into the sixteenth century. It could be considered a spiritual bestseller because it is the most copied of all of the mystic's works. It has been preserved in more than twenty-five manuscripts. Willem Jordaens translated it into Latin, but only a short fragment of that translation has been recovered to date.

Brother Geraert's description is also indicative of the high esteem in which this long treatise was held: "The Book of the Tabernacle praises itself, for there is no one in Holy Church, starting with the pope and down to the lowliest state, who would not gain spiritual advantage for himself if he were to read and understand it. And it also praises its author, since many a subtle spiritual truth has been drawn from complex things scattered over the whole Bible and united in the soul of man, the same way the tabernacle and all things pertaining to it was one piece of work only. In the book in which he begins to speak of the twenty birds God forbade to eat, I have left out an intense attack on all groups belonging to Holy Church. Ruusbroec bewailed the fact that they have fallen so low and keep deviating more and more from the very first origin. But one can find these reprimands in other copies of his books."

Brother Geraert's last remark proves that the Herne Carthusians were less happy with the sharp criticism Ruusbroec roundly wrote down about the abuses in the Church of his time. Great mystics are not afraid to look daily reality in the eye. Saint Catharina of Sienna (+ 1380) freely chastised Pope Gregory XI's behavior and politics in Avignon and moved him to return to Rome. Ruusbroec tried in this way to lead the clergy in these regions back to its real task. It is therefore not fitting to hide his outspoken pamphlet or to water it down. The gift of mysticism does not turn man into a strange creature, divorced from the world, but entrusts him with a prophetic task and a mission to the advantage of his contemporaries.

6

The Founding of the Monastery at Groenendaal (1343)

Let us now go back to Ruusbroec himself who, as a chaplain, lived with his rich uncle Jan Hinckaert. A great deal of his time and attention was devoted to the Brussels beguines, in an attempt to give them both a healthy spirituality and an officially recognized position within the Church. We know that the first beguines only gradually went to live together in beguinages, under the pressure of both social problems and the desire of the Church hierarchy. In 1320 Pope John XXII ordered an examination of the doctrine of the beguines in the Low Countries, and of their way of life. Four years later the bishop of Cambrai wrote an open letter confirming that the examination had been concluded entirely to the advantage of the Brussels beguines. During this examination the bishop's emissaries established a "mistress" as superior of the community. From that moment on the beguines enjoyed an officially recognized status and they were protected against all persecutions and calumnies.

We may suspect that Hinckaert, the son of a Brussels patrician and alderman of the city, was initially less than enthused by both his young nephew's apostolate and his way of life. Jan Hinckaert's function in the church and his position among the Brussels clergy have been described in various ways. According to Pomerius, Ruusbroec's uncle was a canon of the great chapter. This eldest collegium of twelve canons was instituted by the Duke of Brabant in 1047. Next to it, there also existed a smaller chapter of ten canons, and Vrank van Coudenberg undoubtedly was a "canonicus minor" in this collegium for a few years. The archives of Saint Goedele that have been preserved nowhere mention a *canon* Hinckaert. Jan Hinckaert, son of Gerelm, does appear in three documents, but with the title of chaplain only, by no means canon. He probably was the priest responsible for the chapel dedicated to Saint John the Evangelist, until 1337. A document dated June 5, 1337 mentions another chaplain. Hinckaert's renunciation of this ecclesiastical prebend is probably the consequence of a conversion. Pomerius gives us the story in full detail:

> When this canon had lived in the world for a while as those lords tend to do, it happened one day that he heard a voice inside him that said: "Go to the church, because you are about to hear a sermon there that will show you the way to eternal salvation." He immediately followed that advice, went to the church, and found all things there as they had been foretold. He began to listen to the preacher's words with great attention. The preacher had been unable to catch either the right words or the true sense at the beginning of his sermon, but as soon as the canon joined his hearers, the right words flowed so easily from his mouth that all those present were astonished at such passionate words about God. When the preacher himself noticed what was happening to him he did not ascribe the grace abundant of his sermon to himself, but to a special gift of God. At the end of his sermon he told his listeners: "I think this grace abundant that has been given to me at this time, namely to preach like this, has been given to me by our Lord to profit the salvation of one of my listeners, who has heard it so that he may convert and lead a better life."
>
> When the canon heard this he thought silently by himself: "How true the words you have just spoken. God called me here and put words that flow like honey into your mouth to turn me away from the vanity of this world and to convert me to a way of life conducive to salvation."

Whatever one may think of this beautiful story, the fact remains that the worldly priest did begin a new life. He began to regularly attend the choral prayer and to pay attention to the salvation of his own soul. This change did not remain hidden, since a younger canon, Vrank van Coudenberg, joined Hinckaert in his new way of life. It is important to emphasize that the young Ruusbroec did not play a major part in the conversion of the two great lords. Pomerius does point out, however, that the three priests led a pious and exemplary life together in Hinckaert's house, even though each of them kept his own apostolate in his own field of endeavor. "And thus the three persons mentioned above lived together in unity and led a life of great devotion and sanctity."

The three pious priests undoubtedly lived together in this way for a number of years, with nothing to outwardly distinguish them from other priests. They certainly did not suspect they had gradually begun to imitate the real monastic way of life. But we also know that the move to Groenendaal was not decided on suddenly, nor executed without reflection. We know that Vrank van Coudenberg renounced his prebend and his title of canon before April 1339. We may infer this from a document found in the Saint Goedele archives by L. Reypens S.J. in 1914. In this document Duke Jan of Brabant bestows the title of canon and the prebend that goes with it to a certain Johannes de Rockele. This new appointment had been made possible "by the voluntary renunciation on the part of my lord Vrank van Coudenberg, last invested with this dignity." This official document bears the date of April 13, 1339. This document is extremely important to us. It represents the earliest historical document indicating that the three pious priests were considering a new plan. We may assume that the three secular priests had already decided together by then to give up their apostolate in Brussels and to look for a more lonely place to live. The practical realization of this desire was left to Vrank. He came from an influential Brussels family and kept close relations with duke Jan III and the nobles at the court of Brabant. It is not impossible that the choice of Groenendaal had been suggested by the duke himself. In 1304 Jan II had ceded the valley and the ponds of Groenendaal to the hermit Johannes de Busco, a member of his family, who abandoned life at court for the quiet solitude of the Zoniën forest. After his death his hermitage was inhabited successively by Arnold van Diest and by the hermit Lambertus. Perhaps one of them asked Ruusbroec to write down his teaching in *The Sparkling Stone*. Lambertus did not stay in Groenendaal long. He gladly left the hermitage to the three Brussels priests and went to live in another hermitage in the same Zoniën forest at Botendale (Ukkel). In the Easter week of 1343, Vrank van Coudenberg (+ 1386), Jan Hinckaert (+ 1350), and Jan van Ruusbroec (+ 1381) went to live in the Groenendaal hermitage. On Easter Wednesday, April 16, 1343, duke Jan III put the existing hermitage at their disposal, together with a nearby pond and the land bordering on it, on condition that they would build a house there for at least five pious men, at least two of whom had to be priests. The community had to faithfully "execute the divine services to the praise, glory, and honor of almighty God, of the glorious Virgin Mary and of all the saints." Duke Jan made this spiritual gift for the salvation of the souls of his ancestors, and especially of his beloved wife Maria of Evreux who died in 1335. Pomerius makes the pious duchess into an admirer of Bloemardinne's. One way or another, her pious memory moved the duke to become the worldly founder of the new community at Groenendaal.

Two questions remain to be answered in connection with the foundation of Groenendaal. Why did the three secular priests leave Brussels and the chapter of Saint Goedele? What kind of life did they envisage for themselves at Groenendaal? The first question is answered by historians in very different ways. Some assert that Vrank had to leave town for political reasons. Others think Ruusbroec was driven away by followers of Bloemardinne. Sayman van Wijc, keeper of the Groenendaal archives, wrote between 1410 and 1415 that the three pious priests attended the services in the Brussels cathedral with growing reluctance because they were distracted by the hoarse voice of a certain Godfried Kerreken, who kept singing against the measure of the music and below its pitch. Pomerius has incorporated this explanation in his book. Maybe it teaches us more about the care the later Augustinian canons were to give to singing at the right pitch than about the intentions of the first founders. The facts themselves prove that Ruusbroec and his companions were looking for greater solitude in the first place. It is no accident that they selected a spot where a hermit had been living for forty years. Brother Geraert of Herne also emphasizes this desire for separation and solitude: Ruusbroec left Brussels because he wanted "to withdraw from the multitude of men" to be able to lead a life of holy solitude, "because he would rather be free of all meetings." When still a chaplain Ruusbroec had already been described as "solitarius," withdrawn. In his later works he says that the choral prayer should be said with great attention: people should realize and ponder what they are singing. This desire for a greater inner life led the three companions away from the city to the quietude of the distant for-

Poem in Praise of Duke Jan III

And when this third Jan
Of days was a young man
He behaved in such a way
As befits rulers, they say.
His rule was strong and severe,
True Lord he was, both near
And far, of all his land.
Simple and generous of hand.
But all that evil brood
He cleared away for good.
Gossips and those who speak ill,
Murderers and those who will
Beg without need would run
From him if they could. Not one
Promise his mouth had spoken
Would he suffer to be broken
Nor what was written down.
And those who wronged his crown
He would never forget
—His greatest fault, 'tis said—
Fierce against the enemy
He loved friend and family
Set them above all men
And brought them to honor then.
Hunting held him in thrall
It tired him more than all
Who rode with him, or would
Brave danger with him on foot.

(Freely adapted from Jan van Boendale's *Feats of Brabant,* Brussels, 1839, pp. 460–461).

Poem in Praise of the Duchess Maria

I would be remiss today
If I forgot to say
Words of high praise about
Good Maria, Jan's wife devout.
Simple, courtly, generous
True in mind and manners thus
That no one saw her disturbed
Or ever heard a harsh word.
Humble and pure of heart
She would keep herself apart.
In the company of women
She would be as good again
And humble as any other.
About wine she does not bother
She drinks a little, neat
And does not overeat.
She avoids banquet and dinner
Because she has found inner
Peace in her room where she says
The hours. Brabant is blessed
With a lady of such worth,
Praised over all the earth.
Ladies, let her be your mirror
And imitate her honor.
This wise woman, and good
And beautiful, oh would
That God set her soul free
Of all calamity.
She died in the year of our Lord
Thirteen hundred and thirty five
May his mercy keep her alive
Eternally.

(Freely adapted from Jan van Boendale's *Feats of Brabant,* Brussels, 1839, pp. 460–461).

est. Their departure was therefore inspired by a positive calling, a kind of exodus into the wilderness. Negative factors probably also played their part. The cathedral of Saint Goedele was still being built and therefore was hardly an oasis of quiet and peace. Ruusbroec himself describes how the high-born canons failed to act in an inspiring way during the choral prayer: "They either talk among themselves, or they keep silent all the time, or they leave again at the slightest opportunity because they do not find the slightest taste in the service of the Lord." The three companions therefore came to Groenendaal to be able to serve and praise God better and to find more flavor in their spiritual life. It should be realized that they did not want to found a monastery and that they lived the first years without a rule and without a superior. Vrank van Coudenberg was appointed pastor by the bishop of Cambrai, meaning that he was entrusted with the spiritual care of the small group (and of the boars and deer in the forest). The new inhabitants built a small chapel, inaugurated in 1345 by Mathias, auxiliary bishop of Cambrai. The new foundation was therefore a chaplaincy and by no means a monastery. Their endeavor would now be called an experiment. Their bishop gave them permission to go live in solitude for a while. Some of their colleagues and many laymen must have looked on them as priests who had lost their bearings, who no longer knew what to do and who wanted to think about their life in the forest.

It is remarkable that these men, moved by an inner force, did not seek refuge in any of the many monasteries and abbeys, and that they also did not join one of the flourishing beggar orders. It is a fact that Ruusbroec sketches a dim view of the spiritual situation in most of those monasteries. "All orders and religious communities became unfaithful to their origins and similar to the world, except for those religious who do not leave their monasteries or convents: the Carthusians and all the women who live in convents under enclosure. They remain the most faithful to their origins." The three founders of Groenendaal could have thought of a reformed and renewed religious community, but in 1343 the concept of a monastic life was by no means alive among them. They remained in Groenendaal what they were in Brussels: secular priests living in community.

Ruusbroec and his companions did not want to found a monastery, nor did they want to embrace monastic life. For what reason? Because they were not looking for a spiritual institution, but for a deeper spiritual experience. It may be thought that the opposition between experience and institution is described here in too radical a manner. Religious calling does indeed originate in everyday, unordered life, but it usually needs the support of cadres and institutions to develop and flourish. Such is the normal course of events. Yet church life in the thirteenth and fourteenth century in the Low Countries teaches us that different groups of deeply religious people followed a different path. The beguines are one example in the thirteenth century, the Brothers and Sisters of the Common Life another at the end of the fourteenth century. The first beguines were independent women, living alone, without man or rule, but with great religious fervor, who dared to attempt the terrible adventure of a personal relationship with God in the world itself. They did not want vows, or convents, or any special bond with the hierarchy. The same mentality prevailed among Geert Grote's disciples. They did live together in houses of brothers or sisters but without an official, firm commitment. Did they feel too weak and too insecure for permanent religious vows? The English historian R. W. Southern cites other motives for their behavior, and rightly so:

> At the root of everything there was a persistent desire for experiment, a desire to discover for oneself a way of life suited to one's own experience. There was a fear and distrust of the great religious Orders which had claimed so much and aroused such great hopes, only to produce (as it seemed) so little except disillusion. The brethren insisted that they were not hostile to the religious Orders. Indeed many of them in the end became Augustinian canons; but many held out, although the attractions of a binding commitment were strongly felt, especially when a brother left the community. At such a time those who remained felt themselves betrayed, and they looked with envy at communities which could call for legal sanctions against a deserter. The remarkable thing is not that men should have felt the charms of legal sanctions, but that they continued to resist them (R. W. Southern, *Western Society and the Church in the Middle Ages,* pp. 344–345).

The English historian further quotes a letter written in 1490 by a Hildesheim brother. It deals with the thorny question: What to do when a brother leaves the community?

> We are not members of an Order, but religious men trying to live in the world. If we get a papal order compelling those who leave either to return to us or to enter another Order, we shall be selling our liberty to buy chains and prison walls, in order to fall into line and conform to the religious Orders. We too will then be subject to servitude, like slaves who can be corrected only by punishment. I myself indeed once thought that we should accept a Rule and make a profession; but Master Gabriel Biel corrected me, saying that there were already enough members of religious Orders. Our way of life springs and has always sprung from an inner kernel of devotion. (Vita nostra ex adipe processit et procedit devotionis.)

This brother of the Common Life had the same objections against religious orders in 1490 as Ruusbroec had in 1343. In *The Spiritual Tabernacle* we are given a sober and outspoken negative image of the existing monasteries, convents, and beggar orders. "What the founders left behind and held in contempt in the first phase of the order, that is now eagerly sought after by their successors. You can establish that yourself in many ways . . . . They want to eat and drink well and to wear a habit acceptable to fashion. Nothing seems too expensive for them in matters of food, drink, or dress, as long as they can get it. They build high churches and big monasteries . . . . You will find rich and poor brothers among them, just as you would in the world."

Ruusbroec saw with his own eyes that "the world" was rather sought after than left behind in the established religious orders. And should a good man happen to be living in one of those communities, he was sure to be pestered and mocked! True God-seeking people only found lack of understanding and contempt. Ruusbroec and his friends therefore decided to look for a hidden and forgotten life outside of the existing frameworks. They lived for seven years without any legal commitment, neither to each other nor to the hierarchy of the church. Duke Jan III made the gift of Groenendaal to the priest Vrank van Coudenberg. He had to build a house for at least five religious men who would be able to take care of the divine services on the spot. This community would keep the place in full possession. But the community did not have its own statute, nor was anybody really responsible for it. It is understandable that the outside world found it difficult to decide where those "hermits in community" were supposed to fit in.

How would the future of the foundation be assured? To whom would the gift of Groenendaal be transferred? These questions must surely have been alive among the canons of Saint Goedele, who had observed the first three founders living in their midst for so long. Some had a positive attitude towards their friends in the forest, others did not understand anything about the whole endeavor. Gossip and worried questions reached the bishop of Cambrai.

7

Transition to a Religious State (1350)

"In the beginning of March 1350 my lord Vrank left for Cambrai to consult with the bishop about the gossip that was rife. Petrus Andreae had become bishop there in 1349. After a short consultation the bishop decided to travel back to Groenendaal with lord Vrank. On March 10, 1350, Vrank van Coudenberg and Jan van Ruusbroec received the habit of regular canons of Saint Augustine from his hands. The next day my lord Vrank was appointed first superior of the new priory and he was given absolute power to admit new brothers to the community without any external intervention. In this way the chaplaincy was transformed into a priory." Thus far the concise story as told by Sayman van Wijc, keeper of the Groenendaal archives.

Brother Geraert tells the story of this important turning point in more or less the same way. But he lets the choice of a religious state originate with Ruusbroec and his companions, rather than with the bishop. "Moved by divine inspiration they wanted to change to the religious state so that the community would be better kept together after their death, and their foundation would achieve permanence. They took the habit and the rule of the regular canons of Saint Augustine and accepted eight people who spoke their vows in the hands of my lord Vrank. My lord Jan was their prior. They were exemplary in their monastic life before God and men."

Both texts fail to mention Ruusbroec's uncle Jan Hinckaert, and rightly so. Because of his advanced age and his frail health he preferred not to become a full member of the community. But he stayed in Groenendaal until his death, living in the same spirit as the rest of the community, even though he was not wearing the same habit. On the Groenendaal honor panel he is rightly portrayed as a hermit next to the inhabitants of the first hermitage.

When the companions left Brussels they certainly did not intend to found a monastery. How did things develop in that direction after all? This eminently sensible question once more managed to confuse Pomerius the biographer. He cites a number of reasons that have little or nothing to do with the real state of affairs. The duke's gamekeepers are said to have disturbed the quiet of the peaceful valley time and again with their hunting parties in the neighborhood and by demanding that the pious inhabitants supply them with their daily bread. It is not certain at all that these worldly sounds and cares would have stopped once the priory had come into existence. This complaint might tell us more about Pomerius's own time than about the year the priory was founded.

The second reason Pomerius mentions is the ambiguous situation of the first community and its temporal goods. "Having contemplated all things and weighed them wisely, it seemed to him (my lord Vrank) that this new and unusual way of life they had simply adopted would not sustain itself for long unless they accepted some kind of religious habit and were approved by some order of holy church so that their temporal goods would be safeguarded from worldy authorities in the matter of amortizations and that they would then stand protected under the freedom of Holy Church." The first element of this argument seems entirely appropriate. The new and unusual way in which the companions lived together in Groenendaal could hardly maintain itself for long against the pressure of established institutions. The powerful beggar orders fought tooth and nail against any new foundations. Even the beguines fell under the authority of the Church as soon as they went to live together as a community in one place. The second element Pomerius talks about is the amortization of temporal goods. Vrank wanted the possessions to be totally freed from the jurisdiction of worldly authorities and, therefore, also from all manner of taxation.

Pomerius quotes a third reason that led to the foundation of the priory. In 1350 the prior of Saint Victor in Paris supposedly wrote a sharp letter to the companions at Groenendaal to reprimand them for the unusual way of life they had adopted without the Church's approval. We catch Pomerius making a historical mistake once again. A letter was indeed sent from Saint Victor to Groenendaal. This letter, written by Pierre de Saulx in 1366 did not deal with any new way of life, but with the formula used by the Groenendaal Augustinians when they took their vows. Moreover, Pierre de Saulx did not write the letter in question as prior of the famous Paris priory, but as president of the triennial chapter of Augustinians. Recent research concludes therefore that Groenendaal and Saint Victor were never linked by any special legal ties. Groenendaal was an autonomous Brabant monastery from the day of its founding, which is why it became the generally recognized model for new and similar foundations in the Low Countries.

Let us now go back to the question Pomerius answered so unsatisfactorily. Why did the Groenendaal inhabitants choose the rule and the habit of the Augustinian canons? They were undoubtedly looking for an officially recognized ecclesiastical status, first and foremost, because their new and unusual way of life attracted far too much gossip. "Some said it was a group of evildoers but others maintained they were good, pious, and honorable men." Only a foundation recognized by the Church could effectively defend itself against such gossip. The companions' first project intended to seek the solitude of the hermit's existence without abandoning the communal office of the choral prayer. But when they decided to transfer to the religious state they chose a rule well-suited to their past as secular canons. The rule of Saint Augustine was generally observed by canons who lived together. By opting for this rule Groenendaal became a chapter of regular canons linked by a lasting bond to the secular chapter of Saint Goedele.

This bond between Groenendaal and the small chapter of Saint Goedele has been commemorated for centuries. In 1460 the tradition of the yearly visit paid by the canons of the small chapter to their regular brothers in Groenendaal began. That visit always took place on the Monday after the feast of the Holy Trinity. On that day both communities would sing High Mass together in the church of Groenendaal and afterwards they would eat together in the priory's refectory. This meeting was an annual commemoration of the foundation because the first prior, Vrank van Coudenberg, had been a canon of the small chapter for a few years, and Jan van Ruusbroec had also belonged to the clergy of the Brussels cathedral.

This yearly meeting undoubtedly kept the bond between Groenendaal and Saint Goedele alive. This is attested by a material witness, namely the Groenendaal honor panel. Around 1550 the small chapter of Brussels had a painting made for its own meeting room. The painting represented all the great men of Groenendaal surrounding the founder, Vrank, and the good prior Jan van Ruusbroec.

Two side-panels, painted white, are inscribed with a Latin text that expressed the bond between Groenendaal and the chapter: "Ex hoc decem canonicorum collegio originem traxit monasterium viridis vallis in Sonia anno 1343." The man who founded Groenendaal in the Zoniën forest in 1343 was a member of this chapter of ten canons.

8

Ruusbroec in the Groenendaal Community

Ruusbroec made an unforgettable impression on the Groenendaal community. He was not the superior of the monastery and in knowledge he obviously had to defer to magister Vrank, magister Willem Jordaens and other brothers with university degrees. And yet he became the central figure of the new foundation. All contemporaries have the same explanation for this phenomenon: he experienced God's presence in an exceptional manner, he was directly illuminated and inspired by the Holy Ghost and he was able to communicate his knowledge of the divine mystery to others. This exceptional mystical calling was generally recognized and respected by his environment. On this point Ruusbroec obviously differs from other mystical writers in the Christian tradition. Meister Eckhart, Theresia of Avila and John of the Cross experienced recognition in their environment, but also persistent opposition. Nothing like this happened in the peaceful and ostensibly undisturbed life of the Brabant mystic. His life and his teaching mirror the mild glow of a Light that gives insight into his whole existence. The dark night of the mystical calling is only vaguely present as the background of a sun-drenched land.

The good prior was able to share his inner wealth with others. He did so orally in the case of his brothers and the many visitors at Groenendaal. Pomerius describes it as follows: "When his brothers or visitors asked him to speak a stimulating word to them he was usually happy to oblige. Words then flowed so abundantly and easily from his mouth as if he was a vat of young wine whose seams are bursting because of fermentation. Such were the words from his mouth when he spoke to us about the Lord Jesus Christ. Indeed, Jesus himself said to his disciples: 'When you find yourselves in front of kings and princes do not worry about what you are going to say, because it will be given to you at the moment itself' (Matthew 10:15-19). Our Lord said: 'It will be given to you.' He did not say: 'You will have it as if it came from yourself.' Sometimes his words were so fiery they could even move a heart of stone and he could strike sparks from a pebble. At other times not a word would come out of his mouth, even though highly-placed and well-known people were visiting. It then seemed as if he had never received any light from the Holy Ghost. When that happened to him he took his head in his hands to find the inner light again. But if it was not given to him he said without shame: 'Children, don't take it amiss, it won't be for this time.' And he would greet those present and leave."

At other times some brothers would come and talk to him after the evening office. They would then be touched so deeply by his words about the love of God that they forgot time and the (nightly) hour and sat listening, wide awake. And yet they were able to attend the night office fully alert.

9

How and Where Ruusbroec Wrote His Later Works

Pomerius asserts that he heard from older brothers, who had known Ruusbroec personally, how he used to "compose" his books. When the rays of divine illumination washed over his soul he would go to "a secret place somewhere in the forest." He there wrote down on a wax tablet what the Holy Ghost inspired in him and brought the tablet back to the monastery. He wrote his works chapter by chapter, with long intervals in between the chapters. Even though he sometimes had to wait for many weeks until the Holy Ghost moved him to write again, the texts would nevertheless fit together "in good order" and they would create the impression of having been written down as one single whole. This modus operandi may explain why certain thoughts and descriptions are repeated again and again in his works.

"As he got older he could no longer continue this way of writing by himself. But the weakness of his body by no means extinguished the light of his spirit. He therefore took one of his brothers along with him into the forest and that brother had to write down on the wax tablet what the Holy Ghost would inspire in Ruusbroec. In this way he wrote down his high teaching on the active and contemplative life. All people of common sense have to admit that his writings far transcend the faculties of the human mind and that his illuminated spirit has penetrated the contemplation of the divine being just like his patron saint, the holy John the Evangelist, has been allowed to see the heavenly light like an eagle.

"The following story could be corroborated by witnesses who were still alive. It happened one day that the pious prior had left the monastery to go meditate under a tree on a hidden spot in the forest. He was inwardly inflamed there by the fire of divine love to such an extent that he had completely forgotten time and the hour. He stayed away for so long that his brothers became worried and went to look for him along the many small paths in the immense forest.

"After a long search a brother who knew him well noticed a tree in the distance that was surrounded by a wreath of light. He approached warily and saw the pious prior sitting under that tree, carried away, as it were, by the abundant taste of divine bliss. This sign proves clearly that the inner glow of his devotion sometimes visibly manifested itself by means of a miraculous light."

This story of the miraculously illuminated tree (a linden tree in later tradition) shows all the characteristics of a meaningful legend. The material sign wants to communicate a spiritual message: the good prior's shining testimony, visible to all those who were allowed to approach him.

But the sign itself was not forgotten by later centuries. In 1602 the archduchess Isabella had a chapel constructed next to Ruusbroec's linden tree and dedicated it to Our Lady of Loreto. This chapel is clearly visible on the etching of Groenendaal Sanderus included in the *Chronographia sacra Brabantiae.*

10

Groenendaal Writings for a Brussels Poor Clare

Between 1346 and 1361, Ruusbroec wrote four texts for a simple Poor Clare of Brussels, sister Margriet van Meerbeke. Her convent was situated near the Opbrussels gate and called Coudenklooster or Convent of the Urbanists in common parlance, because the sisters observed a Franciscan rule, approved by Pope Urbanus IV in 1263. This rule allowed them to accept possessions and dividends. Hence they were also called "Rich Clares" later on.

The convent of the Urbanists was founded in 1344, thanks to a generous gift of the duke's councillor Willem van Duivenvoorde (+ 1352). On January 18, 1344, Clemens VI gave papal consent, at Avignon, for the foundation of a "closed" convent of Clares at Brussels. The founder had the express stipulation that the sisters had to be "locked in" according to Saint Clara's original rule: "includendae secundum dicti ordinis statuta" written into the deed of foundation.

We do not know whether my lord Willem personally knew the founders of Groenendaal. But he acted completely in the spirit of Ruusbroec when he stipulated that the nuns of the new convent had to live completely closed off from the world. Ruusbroec wrote in *The Spiritual Tabernacle* that very few religious people had kept the zeal of their founders: the Carthusians and also "women who live under enclosure in convents." No wonder Ruusbroec looked favorably on convents that kept strictly to their closed status and no wonder he was willing to assist those communities in word and deed.

It remains remarkable, nevertheless, that Ruusbroec wrote one letter and three important treatises for this simple nun, about whom we only know that she was a "cantoress": it was her task to lead the singing during the offices. Ruusbroec proved to be a very solicitous spiritual guide indeed. The spiritual teaching he wrote down for one nun turned out to be so generally valid and valuable that its original addressee almost became an anonymous type of the honest religious woman.

1. *The first letter.* Sister Margriet's presence as the addressee is undoubtedly greatest in the letter Ruusbroec wrote to her around 1346. The text of this letter was known for a long time only in the Latin translation made by the Cologne Carthusian Surius. In 1964 the Louvain professor R. Lievens rediscovered most of the original Dutch text in a manuscript written in the Saint Agnieten convent in Arnhem around 1480. (R. Lievens, *De eerste brief van Ruusbroec* in: *Verslagen en Mededelingen van de Koninklijke Vlaamse Academie voor Taal- en Letterkunde,* 1964, pp. 211–222.) The letter is very personal in tone because the addressee is often addressed in the second person.

"If you want to belong to Him and not to yourself, you shall be common to all people in their need, but you should not take anybody into your special protection. No confusion or sadness will then come over you if a friend should die or if she should become disloyal and prefer someone else" (CC-CM 110, p. 522). This is the main point of the letter which warns in sharp words against factionalism in the convent. "Everybody wants to attract another to her, and they make the following agreement: be loyal to me and I shall be loyal to you. Give to me and I shall return your gift. Let us stay united so that nobody can separate us: that way nobody will be able to harm us. One will assist the other in every need, both in life and in the hour of death" (CC-CM 110, p. 524). Ruusbroec is very much opposed to such factionalism. He is less afraid of exaggerated sensitivity and particular friendships, but he looks on factionalism as a kind of spiritual insurance policy: the special friend becomes a help in every need. "These people want to come together and talk, early and late, as much as they like, and they cannot bear to be reprimanded. Whoever does so is their enemy. And if they give offense to other people they do not attach the slightest importance to it. It is therefore inevitable that they regress in good behavior and in virtues, both internally and externally. For whoever attracts another human being to herself, rather than show her the way to God, is false and lives in opposition to God's will'' (CC-CM 110, p. 524).

For the same reason Ruusbroec warns his correspondent that she should not tie herself to anyone in affection and desire, not even to her confessor. It is eminently possible that he means himself in this context, since the letter states that he personally visited her convent: ''When I was in your convent last Summer I was given the impression that you were sad.'' We only know of two trips Ruusbroec took from the new cell at Groenendaal: one to the Poor Clares at the Halle gate in Brussels, the other to the Carthusians of Herne. Ruusbroec was willing to travel when the object of his travels was to visit people who had retreated behind a strict monastic enclosure. Other friends and admirers had to come to Groenendaal themselves.

2. Ruusbroec rewrote many thoughts contained in the first letter in his treatise *The Seven Enclosures.* This work describes how a sister is best able to cope with the different prayers and tasks of a typical convent day and how those tasks further help her along on the path towards union with God. The book was written shortly after April 19, 1346, the day on which the first sisters had taken their vows in the Brussels convent of Poor Clares. Ruusbroec wrote out an exhaustive program for them, by means of which he wanted to foster the real monastic spirit in the new community. Strict observance of the monastic enclosure seemed an absolute condition to him:

> Imagine you are asked to come to the parlor-grill in the visitors' room. If you do so eagerly and with great desire in your heart, that is true cause for sadness. For then you are still living more according to the flesh than according to the spirit, more for the world than for God, and you are lacking in the first demand the monastic enclosure makes. For if you like going to visitors' room and if you prefer to lead your life turned outward rather than inward, if you take pleasure in conversations and gossip and news from the world you will not be able to become another Clara, another clear soul, but you will grow darker and coarser by the day. And even if you had felt something about God before, through His grace or through your virtues, you will lose that experience. You will grow dry and empty inside, unsteady and divided in your heart. You will be

> left behind without God's taste or comfort, without zeal or devotion in your prayers and plagued by images inspired by worldly thoughts and other similar vices without number (CC-CM 102, pp. 146–152).

The grill in the visitors' room is definitely a thing of the past now. Convents and monasteries that observe strict enclosure are not. Carthusians, Poor Clares, and the Sisters of the Carmel still do. Such convents and monasteries inevitably create the impression of wanting to buttress themselves against the evil world. Ruusbroec's text clearly describes the enclosure from a different perspective. Possible visitors are not described as helpmates of hell: such an attitude would run counter to the age old tradition of monastic hospitality. The worldly spirit does not enter the visitors' room together with the visitor; rather it is hidden in the heart of the person inside the convent or monastery. The strict medieval rules of enclosure testify to a deep insight into the human heart. That heart remains uneasy, changeable, and ambiguous even within monastic walls. It often appears more sensitive to all kinds of impressions from outside than to the silent touch of the Spirit of God. The enclosure wants to foster quiet attention to what is happening in one's own inner being: without that attention nobody will know about the valuable pearl that lies hidden there.

3. *A Mirror of Eternal Salvation*. Several manuscripts state explicitly that this book was written in 1359. "In the year of our Lord MCCCLIX this was composed by my lord Johan Rusebroec, prior of the regular canons at Groenendaal in Brabant, near Brussels, and he sent it to a nun of Saint Clara who had long asked him for it." Although the "nun" is not mentioned by name, it is very likely that this text was also written for the same Sister Margriet van Meerbeke. Since she knew Ruusbroec from before 1346 it is entirely possible that she had been asking him for this treatise for a long time. The text of the *Mirror* is preceded and followed by a few lines of verse that have been closely analyzed by A. Ampe S.J. He concludes that these lines were not written by Ruusbroec himself, but by Sister Margriet, who had received the work in the form of a letter. Because we know so little about this important correspondent, it is worth quoting her versified words of gratitude:

Pray in true love
To our Lord above
Pray high and low
For all of those
Who wrote or did compose
That we might know
And that those who read or hear
May be called near
The throne above
Where all our family
For all eternity
Will praise God in love.

That we may achieve this
And rise in such high bliss
We ask Jesus's help, God's Son,
That all of us may gather
Before our heavenly Father
And be as one
Where life eternal is
And live in joy after this
When God's reward is won,
Where eyes with love abound
And noble voices sound
The glorious tones.

It is hardly surprising that the "cantoress" gives special attention to the "noble voices" of the heavenly choirs that sound only "glorious tones."

The treatise *A Mirror of Eternal Salvation* is considered the Brabant mystic's ripest work. Small wonder, then, that Geert Grote translated it into Latin. In many manuscripts it has the title *On the Holy Sacrament.* These manuscripts name the whole treatise for its third part, in which the eucharist is treated exhaustively. But the fourth part is at least as important for its own exhaustive description of the specific characteristics of the mystical encounter with God. The word "mirror" clearly has different meanings in Ruusbroec. Sometimes it means just "example." Mary is a mirror for men and women who lead the religious life. Jesus Himself is our mirror and the rule we must observe in life. The treatise, too, functions as a mirror for the reader who can read eternal salvation in it.

The word "mirror" achieves a much deeper meaning in the following passage:

> God has created every man's soul as a living mirror in which He has stamped the image of His nature. In that way God's image lives in us and we in Him . . . . And the life we possess in God is one in God, without mediation; for it lives with the Son unborn in the Father, and it is born with the Son from the Father and it flows forth from them both with the Holy Ghost. And so we live eternally in God and God in us (Werken III, p. 202).

This text does not provide us with a psychological description of the human soul. Rather its religious dimension is expressed. God's own image is present in it as in a living mirror. This divine sign allows man to live in the house of the Father, Son, and Holy Ghost. This divine nucleus warrants the unique dignity of the human person and his calling to keep reflecting God's nearness for all eternity.

4. The last work Ruusbroec sent to Sister Margriet, shortly after 1359, bears the title *The Seven Rungs on the Scale of Spiritual Love*. This treatise was twice translated into Latin during Ruusbroec's lifetime. Jordaens's translation has survived in its entirety; of Geert Groote's translation only fragments remain. The best known chapter in this little book is the description of Christ as cantor leading the song of the blessed in heaven. This text undoubtedly contains a discreet and delicate attention addressed to the Brussels nun, "cantoress" in her community, by her spiritual guide. It may have been an expression of gratitude for the poem Sister Margriet wrote for the *Mirror*.

> Christ will be our cantor who will guide us in our song. His voice is so clear and so glorious and it sounds so pure. He knew the heavenly melody by heart: tones, coloraturas, and trebles sound so good that we shall all gladly sing along with him and praise and thank His heavenly Father (Werken III, p. 258).

11

The Origin of the Last Works

1. *The Little Book of Enlightenment* contains an explanatory commentary on Ruusbroec's first treatise, *The Realm of Lovers.* "Some of my friends expressed the desire and asked me to show and explain to them the truth of the deepest doctrine I have written on, in as few words and as clearly as possible, that nobody might take offense at my words, but that everybody might be helped by them" (CC-CM 101, p. 108).

These friends are known: they were the Herne Carthusians who had sent a messenger to Ruusbroec with the request that he would come to them to explain his teaching to them in person. Although he was already getting on in years by then, Ruusbroec went to Herne on foot, back and forth, and stayed with the Carthusians for three days. He then wrote down his conversation with them, probably around the year 1363.

This explanatory book does contain a new description of the mystic union with God. But it also contains a sharp attack against certain forms of mysticism not connected to Christian faith and life. Ruusbroec again opposes the followers of the Free Spirit, as he had done in the *Espousals* around 1340. Unfortunately we do not know which groups or misled persons were his target. Nothing indicates that he turned against the "flagellants," fanatics on pilgrimage who appeared around 1349 in various cities of the Low Countries and whipped themselves to the point of blood in boisterous processions. Rather his description points to certain circles of quietist devotion, about which very little can be gathered from historical sources.

> These people operate as follows: they allow their body to sit still without any activity, while they remain turned inward into

> themselves with empty and undivided senses. But because they are without training and without clinging to God in love, they are unable to transcend themselves: they just rest in their own being. And so they make their own being into an idol, because they are convinced that they are and have one being with God. But that is impossible. And that is why they are sorely misled, as I have said before on a number of occasions (CC-CM 103, p. 540).

Ruusbroec thought it necessary to sharply oppose such experiences of God on the part of unbelievers or people unconnected with the Church. His own testimony might seem suspect and untrustworthy because it looked—at first sight—so much like the message spread by these followers of the Free Spirit. This might explain why the good prior of Groenendaal subjected false brothers and sisters in the school of mysticism to such fierce attacks.

> They are indeed lacking in true faith, hope, and love . . . . You can cross yourself against the devil, but take great care to avoid these wrongheaded people and observe them meticulously in their words and in their works. Because they want to teach, but not be taught by anybody. They want to reprimand, but not be reprimanded by anybody. They want to command, but not obey anybody. They want to force others, but not be forced by anybody. They want to say what they please, but not be contradicted by anybody. They are headstrong and they do not defer to anyone, and that they call spiritual freedom (CC-CM 101, pp. 114–118).

In other words, these followers of a kind of natural mysticism cannot be converted because they think they possess God in the depths of their own being. They do not accept that God surpasses their own soul by His very nature, nor that He calls His friends to the humble service of others.

Brother Geraert included a good summary of *The Little Book of Enlightenment* in the prologue to his copy of Ruusbroec's works, and he obviously understood its contents well. He shows no interest in false mysticism, nor in the manner in which it is refuted. But he notes, not without humor, that Ruusbroec once again uses a term susceptible to misunderstanding in this explanatory booklet. He and his fellow brothers took exception to the expression "union without difference." He goes on to explain in respectful tones why Ruusbroec resorted to such daring concepts and he offers a concise and sharp-witted summary of the true teaching.

> Apart from other explanations he (Ruusbroec) gives in this book, he distinguishes between three kinds of union with God the human soul is able to experience. The first is mediated, the second unmediated, the third without "difference" or distinction. We object to that expression if we think of the first meaning of "difference," because without "difference" would mean as much as "without any inequality, without any being-other, totally the same, without distinction." And yet it is not possible that the soul can be united with God in such a way that they become one being together, as he also says himself there. The question remains why he calls the third type of union "without difference." Here is my opinion: he called the first union mediated, and the second unmediated. He wanted to put yet another kind of union in third place, but he could not manage to name it without circumlocution and he opted for the expression "without difference," even though that is a little too high to express and formulate his meaning. And so he explains why this term is too high, using the words of Christ as he does so. He prayed to His Father that all His beloved might be one, as He is one with the Father. Although Christ prayed in this manner, He did not mean one in the way He has become one with the Father, one only substance with the Godhead, because that is impossible. Instead, He meant as one as He is one enjoyment and one bliss with the Father, without difference.

2. Ruusbroec's last work bears the title *The Twelve Beguines.* This title does definitely not refer to the book's content; it is taken from the first verse of the introductory poem: *There sat twelve beguines.* In fact this long book contains four different parts that have probably been written separately and later united into an artificial whole. It is not very probable that the four parts have been copied and circulated separately. We may infer this from a letter written to Ruusbroec by Geert Groote in 1381. He says in the letter that he passed a copy of *The Twelve Beguines* on to Margareta van Mekeren, who probably lived in Nijmegen and gave her house to the Sisters of the Common Life, and her com-

panions. But he only gave them the first part because he objects to Ruusbroec's observations about the planets. These planets only appear in part three, which suggests that the four parts were brought together before 1380.

Geert Groote's letter tells more about the circulation of this text during the last years of Ruusbroec's life. The writer addresses not only the good prior, but the whole Groenendaal community. He informs all the brothers of his objections against *The Twelve Beguines.* He advises them to allow only part one to be copied, supplemented with the most useful chapters taken from the other parts. He asks, therefore, that the whole text should be reworked and presented in a different form, if Ruusbroec himself were to approve of this plan.

This shows that Ruusbroec himself did not publish this work, but that the brothers of Groenendaal did. Geert Groote's letter was written in the last year of Ruusbroec's life. Ruusbroec spent the last months of his life in the Groenendaal infirmary and he was no longer able to engage in any spiritual work that could lead to great exertion. It is therefore eminently possible that his brothers collected his still unpublished writings and published them. We have to conclude that they paid little or no attention to the objections of the magister from Deventer, nor to his advice. Whoever is familiar with the medieval mindset knows that everybody was then convinced that the location and the course of the stars had a direct influence on the mood of individuals and their actions. Ruusbroec undoubtedly also adhered to this widespread belief, but that belief did not deny personal freedom and responsibility in any way. His observations on the influence of stars and planets have to be understood against this background. It is true that the contemporary reader is likely to find the astronomical symbols in his argument of limited help. Yet *The Twelve Beguines* also contains illuminating passages that reveal themselves to whoever reads the text with the requisite attention. These passages summarize the good prior's constant teaching in a new and original manner.

> God has created man's rational soul and placed it between the life of nature and the life of grace. This soul is sensual in the senses that are subject to it, rational in itself, and spiritual in its openness to higher things. And these three states form, by nature, one and the same life in man.

> God gave scales into the hands of this rational soul. He put Himself in one scale and His whole creation in the other. He asks and orders our reason and our will to weigh everything according to its just weight and then to choose the best, which is Himself. Even natural reason teaches us to do so, since we are always inclined by nature to look for the best we can find (Werken, IV, p. 160).

3. Ruusbroec left us eleven treatises; he also left a set of seven letters. The first letter has been dealt with extensively in connection with the works he wrote for Sister Margriet van Meerbeke. The second letter is addressed to the lady Machteld, widow of Jan van Culemborg, a knight. These people are difficult to identify in the historical sources, and we do not know how Ruusbroec came to know the lady Machteld. We read in the letter that he allowed her to partake of all the prayers and good works of the Groenendaal priory. The major part of the letter deals with the Eucharist and the life of contemplation.

The third letter is addressed to three hermits of Cologne, named by Surius: Daniël de Pess, my lord of Bongarden, and Gobelinus de Mede. Surius adds that they were three noblemen who had retreated to a hermitage by the Benedictine monastery of Saint Pantaleon. Ruusbroec's letter is a general exhortation in which he confronts them with the heavy sacrifices demanded by the life of a hermit. Reading the letter one gets the impression that Ruusbroec did not know them personally. They themselves or their friends probably asked him for a word of encouragement at the beginning of their new life.

A. Ampe S.J. recently discovered in the Cologne historical archives the contract which the three prominent men made with the abbot and the abbey of Saint Pantaleon. The contract is dated December 30, 1364. Ruusbroec's letter must have been written around the same time. The text of the contract is very interesting because it allows us to focus more sharply on the actual life hermits led.

> We, Gobelinus Jude, Daniël de Pesche and Reynardus de Pomerio, knights. To all who will see or hear this deed we make known what follows. My lord Heyndenricus, abbot, and the whole convention of the abbey of Saint Pantaleon in Cologne

> have given into our possession a few dwellings (mansiones) we had constructed within the domain of their abbey with their consent and special favor, together with the vineyards belonging to the abbot aforementioned, known as Saint Albinus's vineyard. All this for as long as the three of us, or one of us three shall remain alive, to live in those dwellings together with our family and with all other persons we want to take along. We have therefore promised in good faith and promise again that we shall give two vats of good wine from the aforesaid vineyard . . . to the abbot aforesaid or his successors. We determine, moreover, that the dwellings aforementioned and the vineyard, with whatever they may contain, will revert after our death, in the state in which they will then be, to the full and free possession of the aforementioned abbot of the abbey and its convention" (Cologne, Historical Archives, *St. Pantaleon,* Deed 206).

The Cologne document mentions the correct names of the three hermits: Gobelinus Jude (not: de Mede), Daniël de Pesche (not: de Pess), and Reynardus de Pomerio (Surius gives the German version: de Bongarden). It also tells us what the life of a hermit really meant to these knights. They simply went to live, with their family, their whole entourage, and their earthly possessions, in what amounts to guest houses put at their disposal by a rich and flourishing abbey for as long as they lived. These noblemen certainly did not intend to have themselves immured, like the first recluses. They were only looking for a very relative solitude, since they were living with their family and their entourage. The concept of "hermit" had obviously lost its radical meaning for them. The three Cologne hermits seem much more related to the "Messieurs solitaires" of Port Royal than to the first hermits of Groenendaal. The question remains whether they were really looking for anything more than a peaceful and safe existence in pious surroundings: it was good to live under the crosier in the Middle Ages.

The last four letters are addressed to women of different status and condition: a pious virgin in Mechelen (Malines), ladies of high status, and a rich widow. Their historical context escapes us completely. They do prove, however, that the good prior's fame was also spread outside monastic communities. And it was obviously not all that difficult to get the kind man to write a word of encouragement.

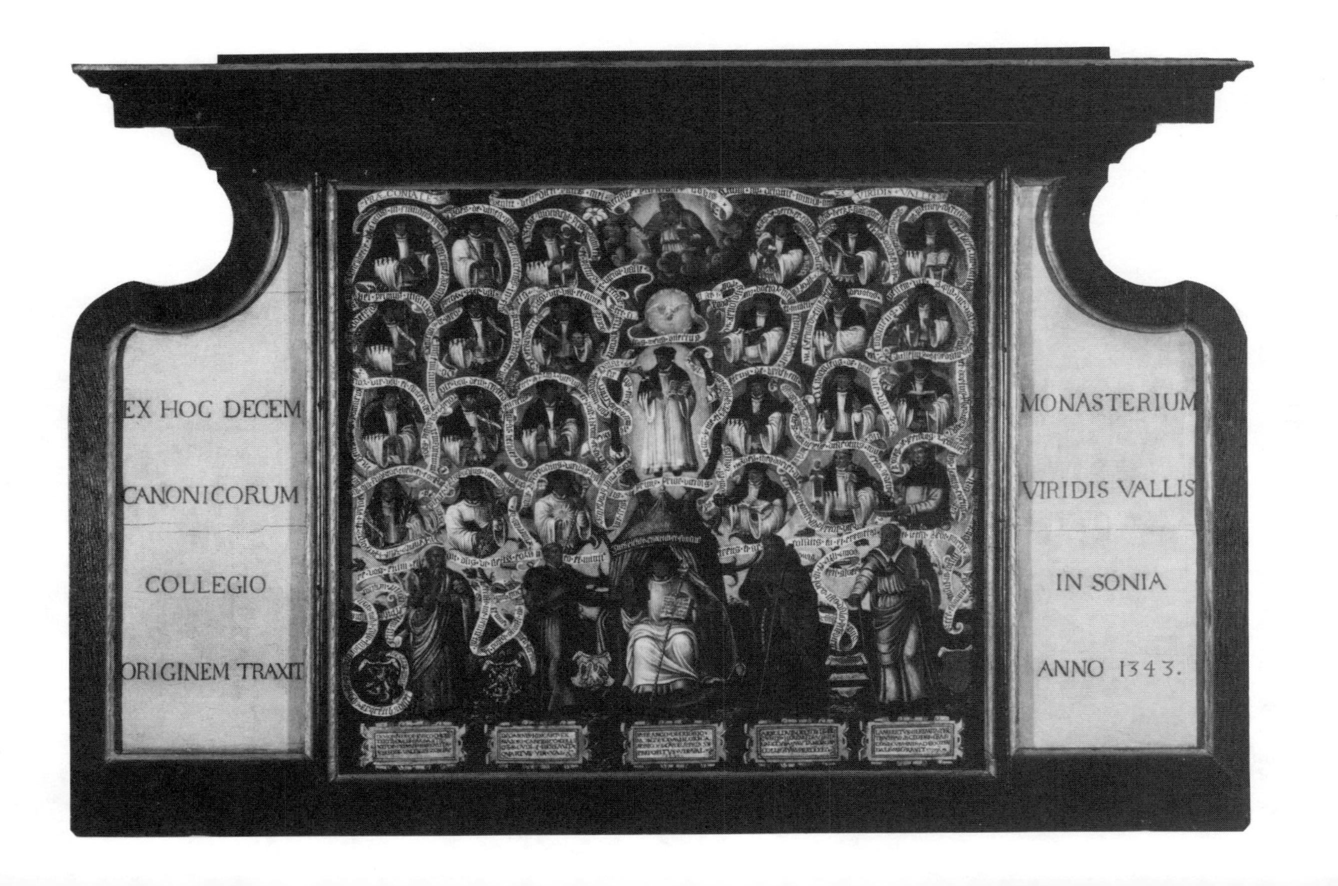
EX HOC DECEM
CANONICORUM
COLLEGIO
ORIGINEM TRAXIT
MONASTERIUM
VIRIDIS VALLIS
IN SONIA
ANNO 1343.

Portraits of the Groenendaal Famous

Since 1932 the Antwerp Ruusbroecgenootschap has had a sixteenth century panel in its possession, on which are painted thirty portraits of men who have lived at Groenendaal as hermits or regular canons. The painting is 66 cm. wide and 62 cm. high. It is mounted in a frame with a cornice and two side panels. The whole frame had been added in the eighteenth century. The following Latin text is written on the side panels: "Ex hoc decem canonicorum collegio originem traxit monasterium viridis vallis in Sonia anno 1343." The Groenendaal monastery was founded in 1343 by some members of this chapter of ten canons. The inscription proves that the panel used to be displayed in the meeting room of the small chapter of Saint Goedele. From 1460 onwards the canons of this chapter undertook a yearly pilgrimage to Groenendaal in memory of both dean Vrank van Coudenberg and prior Jan van Ruusbroec. Jan van Ruusbroec occupies the panel's geometrical midpoint. He has been portrayed in a circle of light. His right hand holds a cross, and his left hand an open book that bears the title of his main treatise: DE ORNATU NUPTIARUM SPIRITUALIUM (The Ornaments of the Spiritual Marriage). Above his head hovers the dove, symbol of the Holy Ghost. The dove itself is surmounted by God the Father, who appears to be blessing the whole congregation of Groenendaal religious.

Vrank van Coudenberg, the founder and first dean, is seated in the middle of the lowest row, under a green canopy. The dean holds the golden dean's staff in his left hand. His right hand holds the scale model of a church which is also supported by his companion on the right (Jan Hinckaert). The Groenendaal church was apparently built at their expense. The other three figures represent the hermits who lived in the Groenendaal hermitage since 1304: Johannes Busco, Arnold van Diest, and Lambertus. Above dean Vrank, to the right, is the portrait of Jan van Schoonhoven: he is holding a burning candle and an open book. Next to him stands the miniaturist Jan Spieghel van Cureghem. Since he is a deacon, he is holding an image of Saint Laurentius. Jan van Leeuwen is portrayed on the extreme right. The good cook is holding a dish with a water jar on it in front of him. In the middle row Willem Jordaens, who translated a number of Ruusbroec's works into Latin, is portrayed on the extreme right. On the extreme left of the same row we find Pomerius, the biographer. Immediately above him we see the portrait of Godfried van Wevel, the founder of Eemsteyn near Dordrecht.

12

The Brothers of Groenendaal

1. The first and most important founder of Groenendaal, Vrank van Coudenberg, lived until July 11, 1386. The story of Ruusbroec's last years illustrates that he was an understanding superior to him. The Groenendaal obituarium describes Father Superior as follows: "How many gifts God gave him can be inferred from the fact that the bishop of Cambrai, duke Jan of Brabant, and the city of Brussels did not dare do anything until they had obtained his advice. Happy the people whose testaments he was willing to execute. Happy the people whose cases he was willing to plead in court."

The Groenendaal inventory teaches us that he favored a personal friend against the sense of his community in at least one case. In this case he was "hard enough on the convention of the brothers, as far as he could." It was a matter of temporal goods he had not always administered according to the wishes of the convention of brothers. Magister Vrank did not leave any writings behind. Was he just a good administrator and a clever man of the law? The fact that he joined Jan Hinckaert in Brussels proves that he was not insensitive to a deeper spiritual life.

2. Jan van Leeuwen (+ 1378) came from Affligem and joined the Groenendaal community in 1344, only one year after its foundation. He was probably a blacksmith before he joined, but became the priory's cook immediately after his arrival and faithfully carried out this task for as long as he lived, which is why he is called "the good cook of Groenendaal." Brother Jan was illiterate when he joined the community. Ruusbroec himself taught him to read and write. Ruusbroec helped him all his life as his confessor and spiritual guide. This nurturing did not remain without

consequences. Brother Jan made great progress in prayer and began to write treatises himself. But they had to be written between pot and kettle, and his writings show obvious signs of this state of affairs: they have little structure, they are loose, and they exhibit a distinct tendency to wordiness.

But these writings are an important source for our knowledge of Ruusbroec. The cook describes his confessor as follows: "I tell you in great truth that no man was better able to speak about deep humility of the heart than my lord Jan van Ruusbroec, my dear and glorious confessor, regular canon and prior of Groenendaal." Brother Jan also provides us with information about two spiritual writers who lived before Ruusbroec: the Flemish woman poet Hadewijch and the German mystic Meister Eckhart. Ruusbroec is often citing excerpts of Hadewijch's works, but he never mentions her by name. Brother Jan tells us explicitly how Groenendaal thought about her:

> Love is by nature broader and wider, higher and deeper and longer than all that heaven and earth can contain. The love of God surpasses all. So also says a holy glorious woman, called Hadewijch, a true teacher. For the books of this Hadewijch were examined before the eyes of God and checked against the teaching of Our Lord Jesus Christ in the light of the Holy Ghost. And they were found to be true and completely in accord with Holy Scripture. Also, I consider Hadewijch's teaching as truthful as that of Saint Paul. But she is not as useful because many people are unable to understand Hadewijch's teaching, because their inner eyes are too dark and not open enough to the quiet love of God.

The Groenendaal community defended Hadewijch's orthodoxy tooth and nail. It would be no exaggeration to state that Ruusbroec and his brothers saved Hadewijch for posterity. Without the recommendation of this monastic community her writings might not have survived.

Jan van Leeuwen wrote a whole treatise on the teaching of Meister Eckhart: "A Little Book on Meister Eckhart's Teaching, in Which He Erred." The great German mystic had died in 1327 and several theses taken from his works were condemned by Pope John XXII in Avignon in 1329. The good cook ventured down a slippery slope when he, an untrained layman, attacked the teaching of the celebrated magister. This is not the place to examine his arguments, but we may infer that his opinion on the German mystic was influenced by Ruusbroec himself. Maybe the cook's judgment turned out to be too negative. The many Dutch translations of Eckhart's writings prove that pious men and women in the Low Countries did not take brother Jan's censure seriously.

3. Master Willem Jordaens was born around 1320, in Brussels. He was the son of Jordaen van Heerzele, cupbearer at the court of Johanna, Duchess of Brabant. Before he joined Groenendaal in 1352 he had been awarded the degree of magister in theology, probably by the university of Paris. Master Willem was held in particular esteem in Groenendaal as the translator of Ruusbroec's works. Since he was a good Latinist, superior Vrank appointed him to translate a few of Ruusbroec's works into the language commonly used in the world of the learned. It has recently been discovered that he also wrote his own works in Dutch, among them a book called *The Mystic Kiss on the Mouth.* Master Willem started his translation of the *Espousals* at the request of the Cistercian monks of Ter Doest (near Bruges). When the Latin translation had been completed it was sent to Ter Doest, preceded by an introductory letter written by the translator. He never mentions himself by name and the letter creates the wrong impression that the translation had been made by Ruusbroec himself. This ambiguity was to mislead Gerson around 1400. The letter is written in very literary language, full of learned quotes. Attentive reading reveals that magister Willem did not spontaneously share the Cistercians' feelings when they expressed their burning admiration for the *Espousals.* But whether he considered their judgment right or exaggerated, he wanted to grant their request in any case. The learned magister dared to sound a critical note which stands out immediately among the general praise Ruusbroec received, and the high esteem in which he was held in Groenendaal.

> To the Brothers of "Ter Doest" in Flanders,
>
> In a humble and pious letter, dear brothers, you asked us to translate into Latin our book on *The Adornment of the Spiritual Espousals* which we published in the Dutch of Brabant a few years ago. You wrote to us that it is impossible for you to fully grasp its full taste because of the differences between the regional languages spoken in the North of Flanders and in

Brabant. Yet the close relationship between both languages did allow you to smell a faint perfume out of the work, and that seemed so sweet to you that you are convinced that all holiness is described in it, yes, even the perfect degree of all holiness, the fullness of all perfection and the final goal of that fullness. Great abundance of hidden sweetness can indeed be found in it by hungry souls and it deserves to be spread abroad by means of the clear light of a Latin translation, as you requested. If your judgment is right, the question remains whether you are not looking for needless complications (by asking for a Latin text), since all you want to do is to find, with Rachel, the odorous mandragora apples (of contemplative prayer). What shall we ourselves say to that? First of all we thank Jesus Christ, who allowed us to share in His apostolic grace and let us be His good perfume, if not everywhere, at least most definitely in your abbey.

Should your judgment not be completely right, you should still be treated according to your faith, since faith deserves wondrous gifts. Things being what they are, I could wish to speak the languages of all people to be able to spread the grace of such an exalted teaching of salvation—those are your own words—among all nations. An effort that can achieve such universal salvation should be called little indeed.

That is why we have acceded to your request and granted what love made you demand: we translated the book you mentioned into Latin, or rather, we put the message of this book in Latin dress. Maybe the book will look changed in this strange dress to those who know both languages, and less attractive. Saint Jerome thinks this is the best way to translate, since it respects the specific character of the Latin language as much as possible.

Dear brothers, be not confused by two structures of language that are so different, as long as the content of the original sounds undistorted in your ears. Beloved brothers, please compensate us for our labor, I beg of you, with the return gift of your prayers, so that we, too, may follow the odorous tracks and share in that perfection of which you, as is witnessed by your letter, smelled the perfume under the literary bark of the book written by us.

4. *Godfried van Wevel.* This Groenendaal canon was born in a rich family at Louvain. He must have joined the community

before 1360, when he was nineteen years old. His younger brother, Simon, was a canon with the Premonstratensians at Park and this Simon translated two works of Ruusbroec's into Latin. Godfried had much to do in Groenendaal: as procurator he was responsible for the material upkeep of the house. He was the spiritual guide of a few noble ladies, among them Maria van Brabant (+ 1399), the widow of Duke Reinout III of Gelderland, who founded the convent of Korsendonk. He also wrote an important spiritual work, *Of the Twelve Virtues (Van den XII dogheden),* long considered to have been written by Ruusbroec himself and therefore included in part IV of the 1932 edition of Ruusbroec's *Works.* This treatise has been preserved in 25 manuscripts. It was translated into Latin before 1400. Yet it is essentially a compilation: much in it is taken both from *The Spiritual Espousals* and from Meister Eckhart's *Reden der Unterscheidung.* Opinions on the German mystic obviously varied widely in Groenendaal.

In 1382 Godfried was sent to Eemstein (near Dordrecht) in the Netherlands to become superior of a new monastery of Augustinian canons. He was asked to establish the choral office and the monastic discipline of the foundation on the Groenendaal model. Godfried died in 1396, probably in Groenendaal. The length of his stay in Eemstein remains unknown.

13

Ruusbroec and the Carthusians

Ruusbroec came into contact with the Carthusians because of the circulation of his works. Brother Geraert himself tells the story of how he happened to get his hands on some of Ruusbroec's books, studied them, and copied them all together in one manuscript. That manuscript contained *The Realm of Lovers, The Spiritual Espousals, The Book of the Tabernacle, The Sparkling Stone,* and *The Little Book of Enlightenment.* It did, unfortunately, not survive. Fortunately, though, Brother Geraert's prologue did survive in other manuscripts and he can be quoted here.

> Although these (books) contain many words and sentences that are beyond my understanding, I still think they have to be good. When the Holy Ghost has clear and obvious teachings written down, we understand them without great effort. But more exalted teaching requires greater effort from our intellect. And if it should happen that the teaching is too exalted for us, we shall then humble ourselves before God and the scholars who wrote it down.
>
> So I and some of our brothers dared to send somebody to my lord Jan so that he might explain to us in person (in his own words) some of the exalted terms we found in his books. That is why we asked him to come to us. Since he was a benevolent man he came, on foot, walking more than five big leagues, even though it was not easy for him.

Brother Geraert admitted that the request he and his brothers addressed to Ruusbroec might seem indiscreet. If we are right in dating Ruusbroec's visit in the year 1362, the Carthusians did indeed demand great exertion of the prior, who was then almost seventy. Herne is thirty kilometers away from Groenendaal, as the crow flies; not exactly next door for an old man.

The messenger of the Carthusians will no doubt have reminded Ruusbroec that the "Carthusians do not go out." Monks who observed a strict enclosure could do no wrong as far as my lord Jan was concerned. He took his time for them and he was prepared for all exertions. And so he walked off to his far and still unknown friends, even though it was not easy for him.

The prior of Groenendaal must have made a deep impression on brother Geraert. The sober scholar and copier seems to have forgotten his many questions once my lord Jan arrived, since he was deeply touched by the welcome visitor's appearance and attitude. Brother Geraert left us the best literary portrait of Ruusbroec, and he describes him as a saint, but a saint described with sober and exact observation. He described, first, his appearance; then, the way in which he spoke to the community; and finally, his attitude during a conversation about his books.

> 1. Many religious things could be written about him: his serene and happy face, his generous and humble conversation, his outward appearance and the religious attitude emanating from his habit and his whole way of doing things.
>
> 2. That was very obvious when he stayed with us in the monastery and we asked him to speak to us on spiritual matters and to impart some of his high understanding to us. He did not want to speak out of his own insight, but had recourse to a few examples and words he had found in holy teachers. With those words he wanted to confirm us in the love of God and make us strong in the service of Holy Church.
>
> 3. When a few of us took him aside and spoke to him about his books, when we told him we had already acquired and copied them, he seemed so free of vain glory in his soul that it seemed as if he had never written them.

At the end of his visit Ruusbroec gave the Carthusians the strongest illustration of his humble soul and his childlike obedience to his own superior. Friendship, apostolate, and mystical testimony had to bend themselves to the requirements of religious discipline. Nowhere else does the Groenendaal visionary prove so clearly in deed that he wants to remain a true son of Holy Church first and foremost, and that he does not believe in a free spirit, cut off from ecclesiastical structures and prescriptions.

> The three days this regular canon stayed with us seemed all too short to us, because everybody who spoke to him or was with him felt himself improve. When we insisted all together that he should stay with us longer he said to us: "My dear brothers, we have to cultivate obedience above all. I promised my superior I would be home again on a certain day and he gave me permission to be absent until that time was past. I must therefore start out in good time to remain obedient to him." We were all greatly edified by those words.

Brother Geraert undoubtedly wrote the most meticulous and the most trustworthy report we have of a particular occurrence in Ruusbroec's life. We know relatively little about what happened later to Geraert of Saintes. A short time after Ruusbroec's visit he went to another monastery that belonged to his order, located in Zelem, near Diest, and in 1371 he stayed in the Carthusian monastery at Liege. He died there in 1375. *The Little Book of Enlightenment* was copied around 1385 by a Carthusian monk from Zelem. That manuscript is now in the abbey of Park (ms. 17). It is plausible to surmise that Brother Geraert took this work of Ruusbroec's with him to Zelem.

Ruusbroec's visit to the Herne Carthusians bore many and good fruits. History teaches that strong bonds were established between Groenendaal and many Carthusian monasteries. We know from an official document that the Groenendaal canons had very friendly relations with certain Carthusians from the monastery of Saint Barbara in Cologne. The Cologne Carthusians were so happy with this that they asked the general prior of the Grande Chartreuse for a special favor for the denizens of Groenendaal, namely that their Brabant friends would be allowed to share in all of the Carthusian order's prayers and good works. Prior William II acquiesced in 1371. In the fifteenth century Dionysius of Rijkel (1402–1471), a Carthusian of Roermond, propagated Ruusbroec's teaching inside and outside his order. He always called the Groenendaal prior "Doctor admirabilis." We shall have more to say about how the Cologne Carthusians helped circulate Ruusbroec's works in the sixteenth century.

14

Visitors at Groenendaal

Pomerius tells the story of two otherwise unidentified "clerks," or religious students from Paris, who came to Groenendaal out of curiosity to be edified by the prior with a good word. For some reason Ruusbroec did not give them much time or attention. He told them succinctly: "You are as holy as you want to be." The visitors from Paris were most amazed at this Brabant conciseness and thought Ruusbroec doubted their good intentions. They therefore told the other brothers what had happened to them, and did not hide their irritation as they did so. The brothers brought them to the prior once more and asked him to elucidate his meaning. Ruusbroec did so with the words: "Is it not true what I told you, that you are as holy as you want to be? Without a doubt. The measure of your holiness only depends on the measure of your good will. Ask yourselves to what extent your will is geared to the good and you will see the extent of your holiness. For every man is as holy as his will is inclined to virtue." The clerks were very edified by these words.

As the years passed Ruusbroec's reputation grew by leaps and bounds, far and wide, not least because of the circulation of his writings. Many powerful and noble people came to visit him at Groenendaal: clerks and masters, young and old. They came to look for light and advice in difficult circumstances, or for a few words of comfort and edification. These visitors would come from Flanders, Strassbourg and Basel, and especially from the Rhineland. Even doctors of theology came "to experience his reverend presence." One of them was a Dominican with a great reputation and great authority. Pomerius calls him "Canclaer," but a later tradition insisted on reading "Taulere." The same Pomerius asserts that Tauler (1300–1361) visited Groenendaal repeatedly and that Ruusbroec's Dutch words moved him to write in the language of his own people as well. This visit of the Rhineland mystic to Groenendaal is not an historical fact. Pomerius' story is not confirmed by any document or testimony. It is possible that later generations may have surmised that both mystics met regularly because they wrote down similar teachings in the languages of their people. The visitors mentioned above are difficult or impossible to identify on the basis of historical sources.

Pomerius also talks about a spiritual daughter of Ruusbroec's, a person well-attested in history. He writes about a woman of high birth, "a certain baroness van der Marck, mother of the illustrious and pious lord Engelbrecht van der Marck, who is still living and has been admitted to the brotherhood of this monastery." This Engelbrecht van der Marck was one of Groenendaal's benefactors. He died on March 8, 1422, and is mentioned on that day in the monastery's obituarium. The text devoted to him confirms the information given by Pomerius, namely that he had been allowed to partake of the spiritual merits of the Groenendaal community because of his many benefactions. The life of his mother, Elizabeth van Hamal, is known to history. When she made Ruusbroec's acquaintance around 1370 she had survived troubled years. She was a daughter of Jan van Hamal, a general of the prince bishop of Liege. She married Engelbrecht van der Marck (senior) around 1356. He was lord of Loverval and a scion of a highly noted family. She was then seventeen at the most, her husband past fifty. Their marriage was blessed with three children, the oldest being Engelbrecht junior, benefactor of Groenendaal.

She lost her husband as early as 1363, which made her a widow at twenty-three. She does not seem to have suffered too much from her condition. Around 1365 she allowed herself to be abducted by her squire, Wouter van Binckom, who made her his lawful spouse over her father's objections. But Wouter soon went on a pilgrimage to the Holy Land and died on his way there. Elizabeth was a widow once more. She married again at the end of 1369 or the beginning of 1370, this time an older, but rich widower: Renier van Schoonvorst. Elizabeth must have been a beautiful and desirable woman.

Her third husband had a vast estate at Saint Agatha-Rode near the city of Louvain, and this became Elizabeth's new home after her third marriage. There began the great trial of her life and there, too, God's mercy was waiting for her. When Renier's children heard that their father wanted to marry a young widow of questionable repute they turned their backs on him and began to harass him in many ways. They occupied or plundered his possessions and the fortune he had amassed with great difficulty melted away like snow in the sun.

In Saint Agatha-Rode the disappointed woman heard people talk about the good prior of Groenendaal. The monastery was only a two hour's walk from her castle. She went there and was soon converted. Pomerius's story of these events runs as follows:

> Although she was involved with the world as her state demanded, she was touched so deeply by God's mercy in her inner life that she would often walk the two leagues from her castle at Rode to the monastery of Groenendaal barefoot, for the sake of the prior who taught her to hold the world and its profits in contempt for the love of Our Lord Jesus Christ. She finally went to Cologne, to become a nun in a convent of Saint Clara.

Her third husband, old Renier, probably showed her the way out of her world. In 1374 or 1375 he left his family and his possessions to join the Knights Templar on the island of Rhodes. He died there on December 27, 1385. Elizabeth is said to have left Rode not long after her husband's departure. Her merciless stepchildren would certainly not have endured her presence in the castle. According to Pomerius she became a Poor Clare in Cologne. A family chronicle, on the other hand, asserts that she had herself immured in a hermitage in Cologne and that she was still alive in 1398.

15

Ruusbroec and Geert Groote

Geert Groote was born in 1340 in Deventer, to a well-to-do and influential family. When he was fifteen he was sent to Paris to study at the University there. In 1358 he was awarded the degree of "magister in artibus." The statutes of the university required that this promotion was not be given to candidates under twenty-one years of age. Geert was only eighteen and the regulation therefore had to be waived for him. He must have possessed a very sharp and precocious intelligence. The young scholar stayed in Paris for a few more years, to teach. At the same time he took the necessary steps to build up a career in the Church. Around 1362 he became a canon of the Aachen cathedral and in 1371 he acquired the same rank in the Utrecht cathedral. In 1374 he became gravely ill in his native city, and this illness was the cause of a radical conversion. Geert thought his life in this world would not last much longer, and began to direct his attention completely to the coming life eternal. He was cured of his illness but stuck to his decision. He subjected himself to a general confession, renounced his ecclesiastical prebends and began a long retreat with the Carthusians of Monnikshuizen near Arnhem. Geert stayed there for two or three years and was led to the insight that he was called to a more apostolic way of life. Although he had only been anointed deacon and refused the sacrament of the priesthood out of a sense of humility, the bishop of Utrecht allowed him to give public sermons in 1379. He became a fiery reformer of the Utrecht clergy and the founder of a lay movement known to history as the "Modern Devotion."

Geert had been given access to the Carthusians' well-stocked library and he realized he would not be able to do without books as a preacher, either. He therefore traveled to Paris in 1378. His biographer says he spent as many gold coins there on the purchase of books as can be carried in a small wine jar. Pomerius tells the story of Geert Groote's first visit to Groenendaal and it is highly probable that the recently converted man of Deventer stopped at Groenendaal on the way to Paris. Why did Geert want to stop in the middle of the Zoniën forest? Undoubtedly to make Ruusbroec's personal acquaintance. He had probably come to know one or more of the prior's treatises during his stay with the Carthusians of Monnikshuizen. Once again the followers of Saint Bruno showed the way to the Brabant visionary. According to Pomerius, master Geert came to Groenendaal together with his friend Jan Scele. As both companions walked through the gate of the monastery, Ruusbroec happened to be the first to meet them. Although he had not seen either of them before, he immediately called master Geert by his name (this miraculous happening is reminiscent of the meeting between Saint Benedict and king Totila), welcomed them both, and took them to the guest quarters.

The visitors stayed a few days at the monastery and Geert Groote had ample opportunity to open his heart to the prior. He greatly admired the deep teaching contained in his writings, but he had his doubts about their orthodoxy. To this Ruusbroec simply replied: "Master Geert, you must know that I never wrote down anything except under the inspiration of the Holy Ghost." According to another contemporary among his brothers the prior replied: "I never wrote anything down in my books without knowing myself to be in the presence of Holy Trinity." And predicting the future like a prophet he added: "Master Geert, you will soon gain insight yourself into the truth of things that still seem strange to you now. But your companion, master Jan, will never be able to understand them."

Pomerius was describing a meeting he had no personal knowledge of. Maybe his story is not reliable in every detail. But master Geert's ambiguous attitude can also be read in his writings. On the one hand he had deep respect and admiration for the mystic, and on the other hand he continually criticized the language and the argumentation in many of his writings. Geert Groote translated three of Ruusbroec's works into Latin, but he did not hesitate to put in small corrections. He sent the *Tabernacle* to the Cistercians at Altencamp and to his friends in Amsterdam. He took the attack on the *Espousals* as a personal attack and rose to the defense of what was written in it. But at the same time he continually reminded his Groenendaal friends of the necessity of textual revision. He offered his good services to help them in this. He also would have preferred to "correct" other treatises before they reached the general public.

How can these reservations be explained in such a great friend and admirer? Dom J. Huijben O.S.B. answered this question as follows: "Ruusbroec and Groote stand opposite each other as the representatives of two opposing spiritual trends. The Brabant mystic has remained a man of the Middle Ages in many respects: his eyes are fixed on the invisible, in the certain conviction that much more truth and reality is hidden in what we do not see than in what our eye discerns. Groote, on the other hand, is the harbinger of modern times: he demands above all a faithful rendition of material reality and has little feel for symbolism and high speculation" (*Jan van Ruusbroec: Leven, Werken,* 1931, p. 136).

Groote grew up in an intellectual environment totally different from that of the Brussels chaplain. But these two great minds did not differ on the intellectual level only. Their religious attitude and their experience of God were also radically different. For Ruusbroec God was the source of joy and light, and the spiritual life seemed to him a peaceful ascent to paradise. Groote remained the convert who gave up his career in the world to ensure eternal life through penance and mortification. This difference in their fundamental spiritual attitudes emerges clearly in a conversation written down by Pomerius.

> One time, when master Geert had been with the prior in the monastery for a while, it seemed to him, after many conversations, that the prior did not have enough of the fear of God in him. He found the prior united so firmly with God in love that he would have just as well lived or died in the name of Christ. He also did not want to receive heavenly joy, or to escape from the tortures of hell, in any other way than he had been destined for by God's will. Master Geert, who still had more fear of hell than love of God, was most amazed by these words. He therefore began to tell the prior with many quotations from the Scriptures and with learned arguments that he

> put too much trust in God's goodness if he did not fear the pains of hell. The prior let this flood of words wash over him, was silent a while, and then replied: "Master Geert, you must know I do not feel the slightest fear. I am prepared to accept from God's hand all that he has destined me for, both in this life and after death. For I think nothing better, more salutary, or more joyful can happen to me and I therefore desire nothing else than that He may always find me prepared to accept His dearest will."

The many quotations and learned arguments had no effect on the older man, who had been familiar with God for so long. Master Geert understood this well and accepted in all humility that Ruusbroec was closer to the Lord and more knowledgeable about His ways. In a letter to the Groenendaal community he asks for the prior's prayers:

> I want to recommend myself for the prayers of your superior and your prior. I would like to be "the prior's footstool" for time and eternity, so strongly is my soul united with him in love and respect. I am already burning with desire for a second meeting to let myself be refreshed by your inspiring presence and to take over some of your spirit. For the time being I have to be content with this hope and I can only express this wish without knowing when it will be fulfilled.

Master Geert testifies elsewhere that the good and holy prior was no less inspired by the Holy Ghost than that great teacher of the church, Pope Gregory the Great. These words were not spoken to obtain the prior's favor, or that of his community, but to recommend Ruusbroec's works. Groote's efforts resulted in the circulation of Ruusbroec's works among the Brothers and Sisters of the Common Life, who must have read them. On Groote's authority Ruusbroec's teaching was vulgarized in the writings of the Modern Devotion and especially in *Imitation of Christ*.

16

Last Years

In the last chapters of his biography Pomerius brought together a number of stories about the great devotion with which Ruusbroec celebrated the Eucharist. From the day of his ordination he saw to it that he could say Mass every day. He would not relinquish this habit, even though he was to live to be older than eighty-seven. Once, when he had started the celebration of the Eucharist, he was so fired by the flames of divine love "that the sensitivity of his outward senses abandoned him to the extent that his nature could not keep him standing very well." When the altar boy noticed that he was beginning to faint at the altar, he quickly called another priest who would be able to finish the Mass Ruusbroec had begun. But when that brother arrived the good prior told him he did not feel ill, but that his inner devotion had become too great, and he himself finished the Mass up to the benediction.

Another time the altar boy noticed that the prior elevated the holy host after consecration without taking care that the crucifix, depicted on the host, could be seen the right side up. The attentive altar boy was thoroughly irritated by this oversight: to the medieval mind the elevation of the consecrated host was the high point of the Eucharist. After Mass everything was quickly brought to the attention of superior Vrank, who had to take the necessary measures. My lord Vrank's primary concern was to prevent this infringement on the liturgical rules from happening again: he was afraid it would cause a scandal and lead to accusations of laxness directed against himself. He therefore told the old prior he could not celebrate Mass any longer. But the prior answered in great humility: "Father Superior, don't tell me I cannot celebrate Mass any more. The mistakes I make while doing so are not due to my old age; they are a special gift of God. For the Lord Jesus made me feel His special presence during Mass and he spoke these words to me: 'I am yours and you are Mine.' " These words are quoted from the Song of Songs: "My beloved is mine and I am His" (2, 16). For Ruusbroec they express the deep reality of the eucharistic meeting and union. He incorporated them into his treatise *Of the Twelve Beguines* precisely that sense (*Werken* IV, p. 17).

Conversation between Ruusbroec and my lord Vrank

I have heard from my lord Jan van Schoonhoven that he heard it said about the prior that the superior once told him he could no longer say Mass without his express permission. A brother who served at Mass had told that the prior was becoming too ill to say Mass. And since the superior was told about these things in this manner he told the prior, when the prior came to see him:

—My lord Jan van Ruusbroec, prior, you are not to say Mass any more.

—Then the good prior asked him: "Why, father Superior?"

—Then the superior replied: "My lord Jan, prior, it is said about you that you are too ill to say Mass and that you might even become unconscious at the altar."

—Then the good prior said to him: "Oh no, good father, let it be, don't tell me I can't say Mass any more."

—Then the superior said: "Good prior, it had better be left undone than done, in case you become too ill."

—Then the prior replied: "No, father, do not tell me I cannot say Mass any more, for I am not too ill."

—Then the superior replied: "No, my lord Jan? Then why was I told so?"

—"Father Superior, I'll tell you so that I may not be bereft of my joy, for saying Mass is my glory and salvation, joy, happiness, and honor. And do not think I shall fall ill during Mass, because I am strengthened by it; and although the brother declared that I was ill, I was really strong and pious and God did my bidding. Our Lord Jesus Christ himself came and revealed himself to me, filling me with a glory and joy that are inexpressible. He filled my heart with such great happiness and joy that I was so enraptured by it and so filled by it that I seemed

> to lose control over myself. And that was the illness the brother thought I had, and the incident he mentioned when he informed you of my illness, and nothing else than what I told you now. Please do not tell me I cannot say Mass any more because of this, since Our Dear Lord reveals himself to me like this, and shows himself to me, and fills my heart with glory and happiness, for it would be too heavy a burden for me to relinquish it." —Look, when that good holy man, Jan van Ruusbroec had spoken to his father like this, the superior replied in his turn and said: "Prior, I very much appreciate the fact that you want to go on saying Mass, as you like, without asking for my permission. And I thank the Lord who visits you and gives you such joy in His fathomless grace and because of your humility that makes you bow down low and allows you to achieve great virtuousness" (From a XVth century manuscript, Brussels, Royal Library, ms. 2559–2562, fol. 279).

When the end of life began to approach for the prior of Groenendaal he was eighty-eight years old and his powers were slowly beginning to fail because of his age. His mother had told him in a vision that he was going to die the next advent. Like a deer longing for the fountain of living water his soul desired with great fervor to meet its Bridegroom and to embrace Him. He asked the superior to be moved from his room to the infirmary because he was getting more and more feverish. After he had been there for about two weeks he surrendered his soul into the hands of the Lord. He died in the presence of his brothers, fully conscious, and without any sign of agony. That happened in the year of Our Lord 1381 on the day of the octave of Saint Catharine (December 2); he was eighty-eight years old and he had been a priest for sixty-four years. His brothers said the usual prayers for the dead, but they were convinced he needed their prayers less than they themselves needed his special intercession with the Lord. During his last illness Ruusbroec was also assisted by a faithful friend who did not belong to the Groenendaal community. Pomerius calls him a great and pious priest, canon at Diest. He was well versed in medicine and came to Groenendaal as soon as he heard of Ruusbroec's illness. He did not want to leave his revered friend's sickbed. After Ruusbroec's death his friend stayed with the other brothers, watching and praying by the bier in the church. As he sat watching next to the body that lay in state he fell into a sweet sleep. The good prior appeared to him in a dream vision. Dressed in sacerdotal vestments he seemed to be ascending the altar, endowed with such glory as cannot be described with the words of man. It was undoubtedly the deceased's way of showing his friend the special gifts of grace he had been allowed to receive during his life while celebrating Mass.

Who was this dean of Diest, who was allowed to receive the first sign of Ruusbroec's glorification? Only the old Church of Saint John had a pastor, who was at the same time dean of a chapter of ten canons. Jan van Herck served in that function in the year 1381. We know he also exercised a judicial function as "notarius" of the bishop of Liege. Pomerius mentions his knowledge of medicine, but this skill of his is not mentioned in any other source. The identification of this faithful friend must therefore remain uncertain for the time being.

17

Veneration and Beatification

After his death, Ruusbroec was buried in the monastery's old church. Vrank van Coudenberg died five years later, in 1386, and his burial was attended by Jan 't Serclaes, bishop of Cambrai. The bishop had Ruusbroec's body exhumed to unite both founders of Groenendaal in one grave, even after their death. Ruusbroec's first "elevation" has been described in a meticulous report. Not just the sacerdotal vestments and the clothes had been preserved, but also the body itself. Only the nose had deteriorated somewhat. The valuable relic lay in state for three days so that the faithful might come and do it reverence. In the meantime a new grave was made ready in the choir of the new church which was then being built, to be finished only in 1395. Both bodies were buried in this grave, separated only by a board. The early veneration that had begun spontaneously was to last for centuries. Even the great of this world, like the emperor Charles V and the infante Isabella came to pay homage to the grave. It was adorned with rich ornaments: cloths and ex-votos, lamps and candles.

Ruusbroec's body rested in that grave from 1386 to 1622. The canons had to leave their monastery in 1572 and again from 1577 to 1606 because of the uncertain situation caused by the wars of religion. When they went back to Groenendaal in 1606 the church and the monastery had been pillaged and laid waste for the most part, but Ruusbroec's grave remained unharmed. As the situation stabilized the Groenendaal canons again began to wish for their brother's beatification. Their wish was shared by the archbishop of Mechelen, Jacobus Boonen, who had the remains exhumed in 1622, so that they might be recognized. All traces of sacerdotal vestments, clothes, and coffin had vanished. At the archbishop's command Lambrecht van Vlierden, a surgeon, took the bones from the tomb and washed them, to take away all dust and earth. Most parts of the skeleton were put in a beautiful wooden shrine. That shrine was buried in the side chapel of the Holy Trinity at Groenendaal, in a stone grave the archduchess Isabella had ordered made at her own expense. The archbishop had seen to it that some bones had been locked in separate reliquaries to be given to some persons or monasteries later on, after Jan van Ruusbroec's beatification. This explains the existence of separate Ruusbroec relics.

In the year 1623 the Carmelite Thomas à Jesu wrote a report on the life and veneration of Jan van Ruusbroec, to obtain his beatification from pope Gregory XIV. An informative procedure was started in Mechelen on January 30, 1624. It seemed to run smoothly and well, also because of the Antwerp canon Albertus Miraeus's active participation. The case was taken to Rome itself, and seemed to proceed smoothly at first, but stalled in 1630 for lack of the necessary funds.

In 1667 the Groenendaal canons again had to abandon their priory because of the wars of Louis XIV. They took Ruusbroec's valuable shrine along with them on their flight to Brussels where they possessed a "refuge" close to the church of Saint Magdalen. In 1670 Amatus Coriache, vicar-general of Mechelen had a new inventory of the extant relics drawn up. The shrine then contained five separate smaller reliquaries and two hip bones. The canons returned to Groenendaal in the same year and they also returned the shrine to its previous location. The veneration of Ruusbroec continued, and hope of possible canonization was not abandoned.

The Groenendaal priory was summarily abolished during the reign of Joseph II, and the inhabitants had to dissolve their community. Ruusbroec's last brothers entrusted his relics to cardinal van Frankenberg, who had them transported to the Brussels cathedral church. The shrine was buried in the chapel of Saint Elizabeth of Hungary. Saint Goedele was severely looted by French soldiers between March 6 and March 14, 1793. The shrine was forced open, the relics scattered and desecrated. On May 20 a report was made on the condition of the church after its profanation. "The shrine that had contained Ruusbroec's relics was found in the canons' room. It still contained the two hip bones, each of which bore the same stamp: a big stamp, black with age, and a smaller one of red wax." These relics were kept in the chaplains' room for a while, but disappeared later without a trace. In spite of all efforts to find them during the beatification procedure they remained lost until 1911, when they were found by accident in a chest in the attic of the Brussels diacony. They bear the stamps described above. Their authenticity was attested by Cardinal Mercier on February 6, 1911. One of the bones is still in the Brussels cathedral; the other has been given to the church of Ruisbroek, Ruusbroec's birthplace.

In the meantime, an attempt was made in 1885 to resume the beatification procedure. In 1888 the Congregation of the Rites allowed Ruusbroec's case to be taken up again in the state in which it was left around 1630. After thorough investigations in Mechelen and in Rome the age-old veneration of Jan van Ruusbroec was solemnly recognized by the papal decree of December 9, 1908. The decree was published in the *Acta Apostolicae Sedis* of January 15, 1909. This recognition amounts to official beatification. The liturgical feast of the blessed Jan van Ruusbroec is celebrated on December 2, the day of his blessed death.

18

The Circulation of Ruusbroec's Works

It is impossible to provide more than a brief survey of the places where the prior's works were copied, preserved, and read. The circulation of the original Middle Dutch text will be dealt with first. We shall then proceed to investigate how the works became known outside the Low Countries by means of translations into Latin and various modern languages.

1. The Middle Dutch text circulated mainly in the convents of regular canons and canonesses that observed the rule of Saint Augustine. These convents originated as independent communities, asking for the guidance and support of already established houses. Eemstein turned to Groenendaal for that purpose and Godfried van Wevel was sent to Eemstein as its superior. This Godfried also played an important part in the foundation of the priory of Korsendonk near Turnhout in 1398. Canons from Korsendonk were later to assist in the foundation of several new houses, among them Bethlehem near Louvain (1407), Ten Troon near Grobbendonk (1414) and Ter Nood Gods near Tongeren (1426). Many convents of regular canons were also founded in the bishopric of Utrecht at the end of the fourteenth century. Soon the desire for a stronger mutual bond between communities that observed the same rule made itself felt. In 1394 or 1395 four convents united into a congregation with that aim: Windesheim near Deventer (1387), Eemstein near Dordrecht (around 1382), Mariënborn near Arnhem (1392), and Nieuwlicht near Hoorn (1392) together founded the chapter of Windesheim. A delegate was sent to Rome to obtain papal approval, and Pope Boniface IX duly approved the union in his bull of May 16, 1395. The Windesheim superior

was to serve as archprior of the chapter. There was to be a yearly general congregation that would appoint "visitatores" to visit the different monasteries. They had the power to punish all transgressions and to eradicate all abuses, both among superiors and ordinary members. The priors had to ask to be relieved of their function at each yearly meeting, and if their resignation was accepted, a new prior was chosen in the monastery in question, in the presence of two priors from other convents belonging to the chapter.

Groenendaal wanted to join the Windesheim chapter as early as 1402. But the bishop of Cambrai, Pierre d'Ailly, would not hear of it because Windesheim followed the pope of Rome and he himself recognized the anti-pope of Avignon. Hence Groenendaal, Rooklooster, and Korsendonk joined together to form the Groenendaal chapter in 1402, which was joined in turn by Bethlehem and Barberendaal, near Tienen, in 1410. This Brabant chapter did not exist for long: the Dutch speaking part of the bishopric of Cambrai ceased to recognize the pope of Avignon in 1411 and this allowed Hendrik Zelle, prior of Groenendaal, to ask to join Windesheim. Groenendaal was allowed to join during the 1412 general meeting.

The Windesheim chapter expanded beyond all expectation. The congregation counted sixteen convents in 1412. By 1500 the number had increased to ninety-seven, i.e. eighty-four communities of men and thirteen of women. There were also many convents of canonesses who did not formally belong to the chapter but whose rector was a Windesheim canon. Windesheim canons also served as the protectors and spiritual guides of the Brothers and Sisters of the Common Life. All of this explains why Windesheim played an essential part in the renewal of spiritual life in the fifteenth century. The Modern Devotion did not arise in its ranks, but the houses belonging to the Windesheim chapter lived in the spirit of the new piety. They became the bearers and propagators of the inner religious life expounded by Ruusbroec and Geert Groote in their books. The manual of the Modern Devotion, *The Imitation of Christ,* was written by Thomas van Kempen (1380–1471), a regular canon of the Windesheim priory of Agnietenberg near Zwolle.

Ruusbroec's works were abundantly copied and carefully preserved in the Windesheim chapter priories, not least in Groenendaal, of course. Pomerius describes how the good prior's treatises were written down. At the beginning of the seventeenth century the Leuven professor Valerius Andreas was shown the Groenendaal manuscript containing all of Ruusbroec's works. This manuscript had been divided into two volumes, and only one of them has come down to us (Brussels, Royal Library, ms. 19295–19297). Its second page shows the well-known miniature that so tellingly portrays the origin of the writings. Various other convents must have integrated nearly all of Ruusbroec's works into their libraries. Five manuscripts containing Ruusbroec texts were preserved in the Rooklooster. Korsendonk and Ter Nood Gods probably had all the works. The six convents inhabited by canonesses who had a Windesheim canon as rector undoubtedly did. These convents were Saint Elizabeth on Mount Sion in Brussels, Galilea in Ghent, the Saint Agnes convents in Arnhem and Maaseik, the convent of Nazareth in the German city of Geldern, and Saint Margaret in the Valley of Josaphat near Bergen op Zoom. The original Brabant text was copied much more often by sisters than by fathers. The latter often preferred a Latin translation, as the Cistercians of Ter Doest had done during Ruusbroec's life. At least two thirds of the manuscripts that have been preserved originated with regular canonesses, tertiaries of Saint Francis, or beguines. Yet the original Brabant text of the *Espousals* had even reached the Carthusian monastery of Salvatorberg near Erfurt.

2. The circulation of the Latin translations has not yet been carefully investigated. However, the Canadian scholar B. Desoer was awarded his doctorate at Montreal for a critical edition of Jordaens's translation of the *Espousals.* He found eleven manuscripts containing that text. Two originate in Brabant (Herne and Park), three in France (Marchiennes, St. Victor in Paris, and Pierre d'Ailly, bishop of Cambrai), four in Italy (Bologna, Monte Cassino, and two in Subiaco), and one in the cathedral at Worcester. This survey proves abundantly that Latin translations had made Ruusbroec known all over Europe. Moreover, the Jordaens text was published in print by the well-known humanist Jacques Lefèvre d'Etaples (1450–1537) in Paris in 1512.

The first translators, Willem Jordaens, Geert Groote, and Simon van Wevel made some of Ruusbroec's treatises accessible to the scholarly, i.e. Latin reading world between the fourteenth and the sixteenth century. In 1549 the Cologne Carthusian Laurentius Surius began a completely new translation of all of Ruusbroec's works into Latin. The scholarly monk's plan had an apologetic aim: the sound teaching of the ancestors was an important weapon in the struggle against the protestantism of his time. Surius's translation was printed by the heirs of Joannes Quentelius in 1552. It was reprinted twice: in 1609 (some copies are dated 1608) and in 1692. This publication made Ruusbroec's works available and accessible on a much larger scale than ever before. Many later translations into modern languages were based on Surius's text.

3. Various works of Ruusbroec's were translated into German very early on, from the original Brabant texts, not from Latin. The *Espousals* were translated shortly after 1350, probably at Strassbourg. German translations of the following works: *The Sparkling Stone, The Little Book of Enlightenment,* and *The Four Temptations* were made in the same century. The last work is often ascribed to Tauler. This early and intense interest in Ruusbroec originated in the circles of the "Friends of God" along the Rhine, whose best known representative is Rulman Merswin (1307–1382).

Long excerpts from the *Brulocht* were translated into English between 1382 and 1408. The translator used Jordaens's Latin text that had become known in England via the Carthusians. These quotes from the *Espousals* are to be found in the treatise *The Chastising of God's Children,* published in Oxford in 1957 by J. Bazire and E. Colledge. *The Sparkling Stone* was translated into English in its entirety at the beginning of the fifteenth century, also on the basis of Jordaens's Latin text. This translation was given the following title in the manuscript: *The Treatise of Perfection of the Sons of God.* The translator names "John Rusbroke" as the author and gives him the function of prior in the Carthusian (sic) monastery of Groenendaal near Brussels. The *Espousals* had been translated into both German and English by 1400. The first French translation of Ruusbroec's masterpiece appeared in Toulouse in 1606, under the title *L'ornement des noces spirituelles.* The title page also contains the following information: "Composé par le divin Docteur et très excellent Contemplateur Jean Rusbroche. Traduict en François par un Religieux Chartreux de Paris." The translator was probably dom Beaucousin, a Carthusian in the monastery of Vauvert in Paris. His translation is based on Surius's Latin text.

19

Gerson's Criticism of the "Espousals"

Throughout his life Ruusbroec was considered an exemplary religious man and a reliable guide on the paths of the spiritual life. His spiritual influence is to be found as much in the writings of the simple cook as in the more learned writings of Godfried van Wevel and Willem Jordaens. His teaching became a guideline for the religious movement of Windesheim, for the Modern Devotion, and for the Friends of God along the Rhine. His writings were received less enthusiastically in France, and especially in Paris. The *Espousals* were even critically analyzed there and condemned as suspect by the great theologian Jean Gerson (1363–1429).

This scholar became chancellor of the University of Paris in 1395. In 1397 he also became dean of the church of Saint Donatius in Bruges and he resided in that old Flemish city until 1401. During that time he came to know the *Espousals* in Jordaens's Latin translation. He read and reread this mystical document with great attention and in his capacity of theologian he encountered insights in it that seemed pure heresy to him. Gerson wrote down his reservations in a letter to the Carthusian Bartholomaeus Clantier, probably a monk in the Carthusian monastery of Herne.

This letter, written between 1396 and 1399 is a long and difficult document, and I can only list its main points here. Gerson first asks with a certain amazement how this text could have possibly been ascribed to an uneducated and illiterate man. The image of Ruusbroec as a miraculously inspired visionary must obviously have reached him, even though Pomerius's biography had not yet been written. Gerson thought the thesis of the uneducated writer could not hold, because the text he read contained quotes from learned authors like Terence and Boethius and referred to all kinds of philosophical statements. Style and syntax suggested human knowledge rather than divine inspiration. Gerson's objection rests on a misunderstanding. He thought the Latin text (including its introductory letter) had been written by Ruusbroec himself, which explains why he could not suspect that style and language were Jordaens's rather than Ruusbroec's. But Gerson's real objections concerned the teaching he read in the third book of the *Espousals.* In his opinion that third book had to be rejected and destroyed (it deserved to be burned) because it was not in harmony with the official teaching of the church.

What heretical theses did Gerson find in the last chapters of the *Espousals?* The heresy of pantheism. According to Gerson, Ruusbroec described what amounts to a kind of pantheistic union of man with the divine being. In the state of highest mystical union man would lose his own created being and be entirely subsumed in the divine being. Gerson knew that Ruusbroec condemns similar opinions in part two of the *Espousals,* but in his opinion the third part still founders in the same pantheistic waters.

This criticism, voiced by so eminent a scholar, could not leave the Groenendaal community unmoved. Gerson's criticism had to be refuted by someone. Jan van Schoonhoven (1356–1432) had studied at the University of Paris before joining the Groenendaal community in 1378. He had known Ruusbroec personally for several years and he had lived in the monastery for twenty years when he was given this difficult task. His answer amounted to a sound refutation, but one that failed to convince the chancellor. Around 1406 Gerson wrote a second letter to father Bartholomaeus, in which he sharpened his criticism, rather than attenuating it. Pomerius therefore twists the truth (consciously or unconsciously) where he states that the chancellor changed his opinion of Ruusbroec's writings and that he came to regard the prior as one of the great teachers of mystical theology.

20

Ruusbroec's Influence on Later Writers

Ruusbroec's disciples and imitators are primarily to be found in the Low Countries and in the Rhineland. This does not mean, though, that the Brabant mystic remained totally unknown to French, Italian, and Spanish spiritual writers. Some of Ruusbroec's insights were taken over in the writings of Benoit de Canfield (+ 1610), Jean de Saint-Samson (+ 1636), and J. J. Surin S.J. (+ 1665). J. Orcibal's research has shown that the great Spanish mystics, John of the Cross and Theresia of Avila were influenced indirectly by their North European predecessors. But these Southern European mystics would read some of Ruusbroec's imitators rather than his own writings. They also reworked the heritage of the past into a very personal and, therefore, original spirituality.

Gerson's criticism had the consequence that Ruusbroec's writings were not widely circulated in countries speaking Romance languages. The Groenendaal prior did not remain unknown there, either, but his authority in Southern Europe cannot be compared to the deep and widespread veneration he enjoyed in the circles of the Modern Devotion, and with the Carthusians and Friars Minor of Northern Europe. His writings exerted such an influence in these communities that a whole group of disciples wrote down the ideas of their master in their own way, and elaborated on them. They can be said to have belonged to three successive generations.

1. The first generation of disciples consists of various brothers who were at Groenendaal together with Ruusbroec: Jan van Leeu-

wen, Willem Jordaens, Godfried van Wevel, and Jan van Schoonhoven. Two writers from the Windesheim community also belong to that generation: Hendrik Mande (1360–1431) and Gerlach Peters (1378–1411).

Hendrik Mande lived at Windesheim as a donor, meaning that he had ceded all his possessions to the convent and that the convent would, in return, support him for the rest of his life, even though he did not take any vows, in exchange for a few small services on his part. He had been a clerk at the court of the counts of Holland. The former clerk kept writing at Windesheim copiously. He is credited with twelve spiritual treatises. He borrowed freely from other authors, among them Hadewijch and Ruusbroec.

Gerlach Peters wrote much less in his short life, but he surpasses Mande in depth and originality. His eyes were very weak (he suffered from myopia), which meant that he had to wait a long time before he was allowed to take his vows, until his good friend Jan Scutken had written a choir book for him with very big letters and notes. His main text is the *Soliloquium* or *Conversation Between the Soul and God.* Gerlach never wanted to write a structured treatise. He wrote down valuable thoughts or insights on small bits of parchment or paper, as Pascal was to do for his *Thoughts* a few centuries later. After his death these fragments were collected by his friend Jan Scutken, subdivided into chapters and circulated as a book. This *Soliloquium* is a personal testimony of exceptional quality. Ruusbroec's influence can be seen clearly in it. Chapter twenty-eight will serve as an example.

> Who will ever be able to grasp fully how the Lord continually checks and contemplates His eternal and indestructible image in us. How He sees and knows Himself in us, because He can be present in us whole and undivided. He enjoys Himself in each of us and we enjoy Him, both in Him and in ourselves. He expressly wants us to resemble more and more the image in which we have been created, because he jealously hunts for our love . . . .
>
> That is why He sometimes seizes all our faculties, not just the higher ones, but also the lower ones, to bring them into oneness with Himself. He then deprives them of their faculty to act, so that no inequality may remain, but so that he may possess us completely and we may be subjected entirely to His handiwork.

2. To the second generation belong Dionysius the Carthusian (1402–1471), Hendrik van Herp (1400–1477), and Thomas van Kempen (1379–1471). We consider the latter to have been the author of the *Imitation of Christ.*

Dionysius spent most of his life in the Carthusian monastery of Roermond. He wrote book after book, with a zeal that could not be checked by anything. In his 169 larger and smaller works he rewrote all of medieval theology. His works were published by the Carthusians of Cologne because they looked on them as the best weapon against the Reformation. Dionysius had great admiration for Ruusbroec's works and he was the first to start calling the Brabant mystic "Doctor admirabilis."

Hendrik van Herp was first rector of the Brothers of the Common Life in both Delft and Gouda. He became a Friar Minor in 1450 and died in 1477 as guardian of the Mechelen convent. His main work, *Mirror of Perfection,* was translated into Latin by the Cologne Carthusian Pieter Bloemeveen in 1536. Herp, or Harphius, to use the Latin version of his name, is so close to the Groenendaal prior in his teaching that he is called "Ruusbroec's herald."

The most widely read and circulated text produced by the Modern Devotion is the *Imitation of Christ.* The original Latin text is usually ascribed to Thomas Hemerken van Kempen, a Windesheim canon of the convent of Saint Agnietenberg near Zwolle. Some assert that there is hardly any influence of Ruusbroec to be found in the *Imitation.* This opinion can be defended only if one looks in the *Imitation* for literal quotes from Ruusbroec's works. Those will not be found. But the fundamental concepts of the *Imitation of Christ* have nearly all been borrowed from the first two parts of the *Espousals,* the parts that deal with the active life and with the inner life. It must be admitted, though, that Ruusbroec and Thomas wrote on the basis of different attitudes. The Groenendaal prior writes from the fullness of his own experience, and his own mystical vision penetrates all aspects of the spiritual life. Thomas reworks the mystical vision into an ascetic path to be followed by the common believer who wants to free himself from the captivity of external things to discover the sweetness of the inner paradise. The *Imitation's* many practical suggestions are therefore closest to the treatise *The Twelve Virtues* in which Godfried van Wevel reworked the teaching of the *Espousals* into concrete guidelines for the spiritual life.

The *Imitation* provides an exhaustive answer to the question asked by the common reader of a mystical testimony: "What does it mean for me in my own life?"

This spiritual book offers the reader a guideline to open the doors of spiritual experience in himself. Hence great attention is paid to devotion as it is really experienced, which is held in high esteem. The *Imitation* therefore tends to be the manual of the loyal friends, rather than of the hidden sons. Yet this practical manual sometimes comes very close to the visionary's message. The thirteenth chapter of the fourth book summarizes the eucharistic treatise of the *Espousals* (*Werken* I, pp. 191–194). Two more of Ruusbroec's fundamental concepts are to be found in the following text: the difference between knowledge and wisdom, and the utter need to turn inward. This text is found in the *Imitation,* book 3, chapter 31.

> Great is the difference between the wisdom of an enlightened man who lives the inner life and the knowledge of a learned cleric who spends all his time studying. The teaching that flows down from above through divine inflowing is much nobler than that achieved by the human mind through assiduous labor.
>
> Enough people can be found who long for contemplation, but they make no effort to exercise themselves in the things that are needed for it. The great obstacle is that they do not get any further than exterior signs and the things of the senses . . . .
>
> How is it that we exert ourselves so much for transitory and worthless things, while we hardly ever think of our inner life, and rarely with our senses turned completely inward.

3. The third generation of writers that lived and wrote in the spirit of Ruusbroec is to be found primarily in Gelderland and North-Brabant. First among them is the authoress of *The Evangelical Pearl* and of the *Temple of Our Soul.* According to a recent study undertaken by P. Begheyn S.J., these works were written by a relative of Saint Petrus Canisius, called Reinalda van Eymeren (1436–1540), a nun in the Saint Agnieten convent at Arnhem. This authoress was linked in great friendship to Maria van Hout (+ 1547), who lived as a beguine in Oisterwijk (near Tilburg). In spite of her withdrawn way of life and her modest knowledge Maria was visited by both clergy and laity and asked about all the problems of the spiritual life. She corresponded with the prior

of the Cologne Carthusian monastery Gerard Kalckbrenner and with the first Jesuits who established themselves in Cologne. Petrus Canisius called her "our mother" and held her in very high esteem. Maria van Hout wrote two spiritual treatises: *The Straight Path* and *The Paradise of Loving Souls.* It is certain that she spent some years in Cologne, where she died in 1547. Five years after her death Surius published the Latin translation of Ruusbroec's collected works.

Ruusbroec's works were mainly read and circulated by the Carthusians and by the adherents of the Modern Devotion. After the Council of Trent spirituality, too, began to conform to the fundamental concepts of the Counter Reformation with its emphasis on the veneration of the Virgin Mary and his devotion focused on the eucharistic presence. Ruusbroec was not completely forgotten, but both the clergy and the laity were more interested in his relics and in the veneration that had grown around him than in his writings. *The Spiritual Espousals* were printed in Dutch for the first time in 1624, and the edition was not the work of the Groenendaal community, but that of the Capuchin friar Gabriel van Antwerpen. Professor Jan David published the first complete edition of Ruusbroec's collected works in the original Dutch between 1858 and 1868. The works have since been reprinted at regular intervals by the scholars of the "Ruusbroecgenootschap," a center for the study of christian spirituality in the University of Antwerp. They have attracted an interest greater than they had ever enjoyed in previous centuries.

II

Anthology

1

The Work of God in Man

> "My *sheep* listen to My voice and *I* know them. *They* follow Me and *I* give them eternal life" (John 10:27-28).

These two verses from the Gospel of Saint John exhibit a remarkable grammatical structure. Both sentences consist of two parts, and the second part mentions the result of the activity described in the first part. But activity and result have another subject. One would expect that the sheep who listen and follow would also proceed to know and find. Not at all! The sheep listen and Jesus knows them; they follow and Jesus gives them eternal life. A remarkable transition takes place, therefore, from human activity and endeavor to an unexpected divine activity. The evangelist starts out with human longing, but his real message concerns the knowledge God possesses, His love and His gift of eternal life.

This transition from a human to a divine perspective occurs with great frequency in Ruusbroec's writings. The result is that Ruusbroec often transcends the level of psychological experience. He rarely described his direct personal experience. We possess no spiritual diary written by him comparable to those of Dietrich Bonhoeffer, Dag Hammerskjöld, Charles de Foucauld, or Thérèse of Lisieux. Human curiosity is directed more towards the way the experience of God is colored by specific people, than to the divine message itself. That is why the modern reader prefers a spiritual biography to a book like *The Imitation of Christ* and even to the Scriptures themselves. But the same modern reader sometimes focuses on the idea that every biography is very much tied to concrete situations and coincidences. The deepest experiences and the most personal decisions are caught in a web of causes and effects. At the end of the story the book is put away on its shelf and the reader moves on to the day's agenda.

Like John the Evangelist, Ruusbroec always tries to follow actual experience and to describe it in depth. In doing so, he pays more attention to divine activity than to the many aspects of human psychology. Such a description is more objective than a personal testimony. This sober objectivity calls for the reader's own empathy. He is confronted with the depth and mystery of his own life, rather than with the writer's high mystical experiences. The reader is therefore invited to recognize God's light and work in his own life. Ruusbroec does not do this by means of a moralizing sermon, but through the description of God's actions in man's feeling and intellect.

> The second river originates in man's love and God's loyalty: it is a spiritual clarity that flows into the intellect and illuminates it in many ways. But that light escapes our effort. For even though we always possess that light in our soul, it is God who makes it speak or keep silent. He can show it to us or hide it from us, give it or take it away, where and when He wants to. For that light is His; that is why He gives it when He wants to, and where He wants to, and for whom He wants to (CC-CM 103, pp. 402–404).

Ruusbroec says elsewhere that the light reveals itself when man least suspects or expects it. This divine light is not the result of human thinking and meditation. The clarity with which this light inundates the soul transcends human intelligence. It is beyond human reason, but it does not leave reason untouched, since rational man wants to come to an ever deeper awareness and understanding of what happens to him so unexpectedly. So spiritual man grows towards the contemplation of God's light through God's own light and God's own effort.

> The spirit raises itself up through illuminated reason and directs its eyes and its thoughts towards the innermost part of his spirit, where God is at work. Here reason and all created light are of no avail to further progress, because divine clarity blinds all created sight by its own arrival. And all understanding in cre-

ated light behaves in this like the eye of a bat in the shining of the sun.

And yet the spirit is always again compelled and invited to fathom the deeply hidden workings of God, to get to know what God is and what his work consists of. Illuminated reason keeps asking itself new questions as to where this may be coming from and tries to exploit that vein of honey (i.e. God's presence) down to its deepest depth. But it never grows any wiser than on the first day. That is why reason and intellect confess: "I do not know what it is."

But where reason and intellect fear when confronted with divine clarity, and stand outside the gate, *love's desire wants to go beyond* since it, too, is invited and compelled, just as the intellect is. But love is blind and wants to enjoy above all. This enjoyment, however, consists more in tasting and in feeling than in understanding. That is why love wants to enter where the intellect stays outside (CC-CM 103, p. 456).

2

The Three Stages of Spiritual Life

In his masterpiece, *The Spiritual Espousals,* Ruusbroec distinguishes three stages in the growth of spiritual life. Whoever wants to seriously live his faith must first exercise himself in the virtues of the active life. That is followed by the interiorization of the life that desires God, and finally by the loving union of the life that contemplates God. This representation of spiritual growth and progress may create the impression that Ruusbroec regards the mystical life as the normal crowning of a successful religious life. But our Brabant mystic has too much common sense to posit such a controversial thesis. The facts themselves would refute such an opinion. The Church reveres many saints who definitely never reached the highest mystical contemplation of God in this world. On the other hand, many mystics testify that they did not receive their highest mystic gifts at the end of their spiritual adventure, but at the beginning of it, and in a totally unexpected and irresistible way.

Nowhere did Ruusbroec better describe the specific nature of the mystical calling than in the first part of his little book *The Sparkling Stone.* Brother Geraert, the Carthusian of Herne, tells us that this small treatise was written by Ruusbroec after a long spiritual conversation with an unknown hermit. This pious God-seeking man was so overjoyed by the spiritual conversation that he asked the good prior to write down the teaching he had given him by means of the spoken word. This little book summarizes the high teaching of the *Espousals* in very simple language. The chapter on the four kinds of good people in particular is a masterpiece of spiritual psychology and absolute clarity. Ruusbroec exhibits great respect for everybody's personal calling in these pages, and his mild eye is able to hold every profession and every state in the highest esteem. This is how he points out the difference between hired hands, faithful servants, secret friends, and hidden sons.

On four kinds of "good people"

That is why we must direct our eyes to God and see how He calls all men in free goodness, without distinction, good men as well as evil, nobody excepted, and invites them to oneness with Him. Secondly we must consider how the goodness of God flows out into all people who answer God's call. Thirdly we must clearly and distinctly experience and understand in ourselves that we can become one life and one spirit with God if we renounce ourselves in all respects and follow the grace of God in towards the highest point where it wants to lead us. For the grace of God works in all men in an *orderly* manner, according to the measure and the manner of his ability to receive it.

All that we are and all that we have received, inwardly and outwardly, are all free gifts of God for which we have to thank Him and with which we have to serve Him if we want to please Him. There are many gifts of God that are a help to good people and an occasion to practice virtue; for those who are evil, on the other hand, they are a help and an occasion to sin, such as health, beauty, wisdom, wealth, and a good reputation in the world. These are the lowest and least valuable gifts God gives to all men, to benefit both His friends and His enemies, both good men and evil. And with them good men serve God and His friends; evil men serve their own flesh, the devil, and the world.

1. Hired hands and faithful servants

We can further see that some people receive the gifts of God like hired hands of God, and others like faithful servants. Both groups are different both in their love and in their intention, both in their feelings and in all the inner works and exercises of their life.

Mark the following well: all people who love themselves so beyond all measure that they do not want to serve God in any other way than for their own gain and profit, keep themselves

> at a distance from God and remain unfree, caught in their love of self. For they are looking for themselves and are their own goal in all they do and leave undone. That is why they only strive after temporal things with all their prayers and good works, or if they strive after eternal things they do so only for their own benefit and advantage. These people are attached to themselves beyond measure and that is why they always remain alone with themselves, for honest love that would unite them with God and with all His loved ones is lacking in them. And even if these people seem to observe the law of God and Holy Church they do not observe the law of love! For they do whatever they do out of a sense of obligation and not out of love, namely in order not to be damned. And because they are, in fact, inwardly unfaithful, they dare not trust in God. On the contrary, all their inner life is doubt and fear, hardship and wretchedness. For they see eternal life on the right hand side, and that they are afraid to lose, and on the left hand side the eternal torments of hell, and those they are afraid to get. All the praying, all the labor, and all the good works they do to chase this fear away are of no use to them whatsoever. For the more they love themselves beyond measure, the more they are also afraid of hell. And from this you may conclude that this fear of hell originates in the love they nurture for themselves (CC-CM 110, pp. 122–126).

The hired hands act as merchants in the market place of spiritual life. In their relationship to God they observe the same principles and the same laws as in their worldly activities: they do not want to serve God in any other way than for their own profit and gain. Ruusbroec does not assert here that God holds such mercenary worship in contempt. On the contrary, he shows great respect for every man's own calling and typical life history. Yet our spiritual guide has a sharp eye for the shortcomings of this self-serving worship. Those who honor God in this way mislead and delude themselves. Their worship is not directed towards God, but towards themselves, because they are looking for themselves in all they do and leave undone. Such believers keep themselves at a distance from God and stay caught in their love of self. Even their fear of hell locks them deeper away within the narrow walls of that love of self. Only real faith can break open the prison of human loneliness. That is why Ruusbroec places little trust in a religious attitude that originates in force or fear. His faith is not in a God of revenge and punishment, against whom man has to arm himself as well as he can. Calvin's punishing God is unknown to him, as is the divine moralist of the Jansenists.

2. *Faithful servants and secret friends*

We can further find a big difference between the faithful servants of God and His secret friends. With the help of God's grace the faithful servants are fully determined to observe the commandments, that is: to be obedient to God and to Holy Church in all kinds of virtues and good manner of life. That is called an exterior or active life. The secret friends, however, prefer to keep God's living counsel as well as His commandments, that is: a loving inner cleaving to God for His eternal honor's sake, together with the willing renunciation of all one could possess outside of God with joy and love. God calls such friends and invites them inward and He gives them insight in the inner exercises and in the many different and hidden paths of spiritual life. But His servants He sends outward, that they may remain faithful to Him and His family (Christianity) in all kinds of services and in all kinds of external good works.

So God gives His help and His grace according to each man's ability, that is: the way in which each man adapts himself to God's will, be it in external good works, or in internal exercises of love. But nobody can be busy with internal exercises, or experience anything internally if he has not turned towards God wholly and completely.

As long as man is divided in his heart, he remains turned outward and unsteady in his soul, and he is easily moved by good and bad in temporal things because those are still alive in him. And, though he lives according to God's commands, he remains unilluminated and untaught inside because he does not know what inner exercises mean, nor how he should apply himself to them. As long as he knows and feels that he means well with God, and if he tries to carry out God's dearest wish in all his works, he is content because then he sees a pure intention in his life, and loyal service. He pleases himself on those two accounts. And it seems to him that exterior good works, done with honest intention, are holier and more useful than inner exercises because he has, with God's help, chosen an external way of life. This is why he pays more attention to external works

> of all kinds than to Him for Whom he is working with ardent love. This is why his spirit is more occupied with the works he does, than with God for Whom he does them. Because he loses himself in his activities, he remains an external man, and he is not able to follow God's counsel because his activities are more external than internal, more material than spiritual. And even though he is a faithful servant of God through his external service, what the Creator's intimate friends experience remains hidden to him . . . . And so you know the difference between the faithful servants and the secret friends of our Lord (CC-CM 110, pp. 128–132).

The hired hands look for their own gain and their own profit in the faith, more than for the honor and glory of God. The faithful servants, on the other hand, try to carry out God's dearest wish with unfeigned good intentions and with true loyalty. Ruusbroec's choice of words proves that he has great respect for such faithful servants. They live an exemplary life according to the demands of their specific calling: to do all kinds of good works and to render as much service as possible to God and His family in this world. This charisma of good works seems to be a lasting characteristic of the Christian community. It is given a distinct image in the seven physical works of mercy that have been represented in a unique manner on the splendid altarpiece of the Master of Alkmaar, now in the Rijksmuseum in Amsterdam. The seven works are represented there on as many panels: to feed the hungry, to give drink to the thirsty, to clothe the naked, to give shelter to strangers, to visit the sick, to free the prisoners, and to bury the dead. Whoever looks attentively at these panels will notice that the same face of Jesus has been painted unobtrusively among the hungry and the thirsty, the naked and the sick, the strangers and the prisoners. The faithful servants, male and female, care with one and the same deed both for Christ and for His family in this world. And yet Ruusbroec asserts that there is another and deeper calling than this active apostolate. That special calling of the secret friends is specified more and more in Ruusbroec's description. We read first that the friends want to observe God's living counsel as well as His commandments. It is remarkable that Ruusbroec should speak of God's *counsel* (in the singular), and not of the three well-known evangelical counsels. He is, therefore, not referring to the religious life with its vows of poverty, chastity, and obedience. God's living counsel does not bring the friends to a traditional monastic or religious order, but invites them to a special bond with God! They prefer a loving inner cleaving to God, together with the willing renunciation of all they might be able to desire and possess in this world—outside of God. This calling to a more inward faith made Ruusbroec move from the bustle of the city to the lonely silence of Groenendaal. The secret friends are invited to an inner, or ardent life. In this their spirit leaves the colorful kaleidoscope of the external world, to penetrate to the ground of their own being, where they find God. The servant is completely faithful if he keeps looking for God's will and tries to carry it out in all his works. Because he loses himself in his works, because of the worries of a busy apostolate, the servant remains an external man. The secret friend is not called to action in the first place, but to prayer and turning inward. Nobody can apply himself to such inner exercises if he does not totally direct his attention towards the love of God that invites him and recruits him. The friends take care that those works do not take up too much of their time and attention, because they want to keep directing their spirit towards the divine Master first of all, and they think His presence is more important than all they themselves are able to achieve.

3. Secret friends and hidden sons

We find an even deeper and more subtle difference between the secret friends and the hidden sons of God. Both groups have developed an attentive alertness to the presence of God by means of ardent exercises, but the friends still have some self-will in their inner life, because they consider loving commerce with God the best and the very highest they can or want to reach. And that is why they are unable to transcend themselves or their works to make themselves totally empty for God's presence. They themselves and their works constitute a mediatedness and an image between themselves and God. And although they feel a certain union with God as they cling to Him in love, they also always feel distinction and otherness between themselves and God within that union.

Although they possess a clear understanding and discernment of all reasonable virtues, the simple contemplation with open mind in divine clarity remains hidden from them. Although they

> feel attracted to God by a strong fire of love, they still maintain their self-will and are not consumed, not burned completely (like a sacrificial victim) in the unity of love. Although they want to serve God always and please Him for ever, they do not want to die to all self-will of spirit in God, nor lead the life that is His. And although they attach little importance to all comfort and all rest that comes from outside, they attach great importance to God's gifts, to their own inner works, and to the comfort and sweetness they feel inside. And so they tarry by the wayside and do not die so completely that they gain the highest victory through self-denying abandon. And even if they were to exercise all manner of love and to take all the paths of inner ascent one walks before the presence of God, the total surrender and the rich wandering in the divine love itself, to which one can never find end nor beginning, way nor manner, would remain hidden and unknown to them (CC-CM 110, pp. 134–136).

In this chapter Ruusbroec deals with the difference between two groups of people who live the inner life in the love of God. He writes about two groups within religious life. Yet his attention is not devoted to the characteristics of the *group,* but to the difference in *personal* experience. The same ardent man can first act as a friend and then experience the grace of the full status of son.

The soul in search can enter into a relationship with God in two ways. In the first way man looks *actively* for God's nearness in work and prayer. He tries to look more and more like the Beloved and experiences a certain union with God in and through his works. But no man will achieve true unity with Him at Whom his whole desire is aimed in this way. That unity can only be experienced if the same man allows himself to be *passively* approached and transformed by the activity of God's Holy Spirit.

> Our activity always keeps us on the level of becoming equal. We experience that our search and contemplation go out to Someone who is greater than all we are. In that way we can begin to resemble God. But where God Himself is at work we are shaped by His Spirit, we are subjected to the transformation effected by His clarity and love. There we are the sons of God in grace, beyond all likeness (*Werken* III, pp. 207–208).

Why is there such a fundamental difference between "likeness" and "unity" in the relationship between man and his Creator?

This question touches the very essence of the mystical experience. P. Mommaers S.J. has summarized Ruusbroec's answer as follows.

> No matter how far the likeness with God can reach, it never becomes unity with Him. Why should that be? Because growing alike always happens in a *certain manner,* according to the peculiar and individual manner of him who becomes alike. I can probably imitate in a perfect way, become as perfect an image of the Other as possible, but that alone is never being one, because I am the one who takes over and makes the Other mine. I remain the principle of my life in likeness. My self-will remains untouched, it is even reinforced in a certain way, and the separation from the Other continues. Being alike never succeeds in breaking through loneliness. That is also why Ruusbroec says that becoming one, as such, has to happen "without any manner," undefined. As long as I am there in my special manner and the Other has to be appropriated by me according to my special manner of becoming one, there can be no true unity. I may become more and more like Him, but He can only be experienced in Himself as the Other (P. Mommaers, *The Land Within,* Chicago, 1975, p. 82).

This openness to the coming of the Other is experienced as an enormous risk, as a leap into the dark, as a deadly fall into burning oil that consumes everything. Ruusbroec refers to it by using the image of the sacrificial lamb on the pyre, that is completely *burnt up* and consumed. Only in that glow are the joy and the blessedness of unity in love experienced.

> Where the human spirit turns consciously into itself, it notices distinction and otherness between itself and God. But where it burns up it is onefold and does not experience distinction: there it feels nothing but unity. For the eternal flame of the love of God consumes and devours all it can seize in its Selfhood. That devouring unity is nothing but the fathomless love that pulls the Father and the Son and all who live in Him inward into an eternal enjoyment. In this love we want to burn and be burnt without end for all eternity, because in it all spirits experience perfect blessedness (*Werken* III, p. 8).

3

A Hymn to Holy Trinity

The following text allows us to empathize with the way in which the theoretical content of the doctrine of the faith becomes living reality for the visionary. The doctrine of the one divine nature in three Persons is then no longer accepted on the authority of Holy Church or Holy Scripture, but the divine mystery reveals itself directly before the inner eye of the loving soul. Moreover, the glow of the godhead spreads itself over the whole visible creation.

> Christ expects the man who has been illuminated by him to go out (like the wise virgins with their oil) and to behave in that light after the manner of shining light. . . . In this the nature of the godhead reveals itself as simplicity and one-foldness, as inaccessible height and abyss-like depth, as incomprehensible breadth and endless length, a dark stillness and a wild desert, the repose of all the saints in unity, a common enjoyment of Itself and of all the saints in eternity. And one can contemplate many more wondrous things in that bottomless sea of the godhead.
>
> The illuminated man will also consider and contemplate the quality of the *Father* in the godhead. His almighty power and majesty, because He is creator, sustainer, mover, beginning and end, the cause and "first principle" of all creatures.
>
> The illuminated man also sees the attributes of the eternal *Word:* its unfathomable wisdom and truth, the primal image and life-source of all creatures, eternal and unchangeable rule, an intent seeing and an unscreened penetrating vision of all

things, an enlightenment of all the saints in heaven and on earth according to their dignity.

Illuminated reason also sees the attributes of the *Holy Spirit:* incomprehensible charity and generosity, mercy and clemency, endless loyalty and graciousness, incomprehensible and great outflowing riches and an abyss-like goodness that overwhelms all celestial spirits with blissfulness. He is a blazing flame that consumes all of creation in one unifying glow, a fountain that runs over, rich with every savor according to everyone's desire. He prepares all saints and leads them into their eternal blessedness: the mutual embracing and possessing in love of Father and Son and all the saints in enjoyable unity.

The incomprehensible richness and the sublimity of divine nature strike man with amazement. And what is most amazing is the commonness of God and most of all His outflowing. For he sees this incomprehensible Being as a common enjoyment of God and all the saints. And he sees how the divine Persons flow out in a common manner and work in heaven and on earth, in nature and above nature, in all places and at all times, in the saints in heaven and in men on earth, in all creatures, both rational and non-rational and even purely material, according to each one's worthiness and need and receptivity.

When man sees the wondrous riches like this, the sublimity of the divine nature and all the manifold gifts God wants to offer His creatures, there grows within him an astonishment about God's riches, so great and manifold, and about the unending loyalty He shows His creatures. From this springs in the human spirit an unspeakable inward joy and a great trust in God. And this inward joy embraces and permeates all the faculties of the soul, as well as the unity of the spirit (CC-CM 103, pp. 404–414).

4

What the Senses Experience During the Encounter with God

In the *Espousals* Ruusbroec describes the gift of divine inebriation in a very penetrating manner. He may have been influenced by the text of Cardinal Jacobus of Vitry (1170–1240), cited below. He may also speak out of his own experience and observation. In any case the mystic testifies that the coming of Christ to the loving heart can entail very strong physical reactions. These experiences of the senses do not belong to the nucleus of the encounter with God, but they are described and valued in a positive way in the text that follows. Those who experience God are sometimes also allowed to feel in their bodies how pleasant and blissful it is to be with Him. The spiritual experience cannot be considered as non-physical and the religious man does not have to renounce his senses. Ruusbroec does not mean by this that the senses can be allowed free play, nor that physical experiences inevitably open the door to the realm of the Spirit. But Christ approaches man as a being of flesh and blood.

> There is still another coming of Christ to the loving heart and that is experienced in great sweetness. This sweetness awakens a blissfulness in the heart and in all faculties of the body, so that it appears to man as if he is inwardly embraced and enveloped by God's love. This bliss and this comfort are greater and more enjoyable for body and soul than all the earth can provide of pleasure and satisfaction, even were a man able to receive them all at once. In this blissfulness God Himself descends into the heart through His gifts with so much taste and com-

fort and joy that the heart overflows within. This makes man understand how wretched all those are who dwell outside of love. This blessed feeling is called the flowing-away of the heart, so that man can not restrain himself because of the fullness of inward joy.

Out of this bliss comes spiritual drunkenness. Spiritual drunkenness means that man receives more sensible relish and well-being than his heart or his desire can either desire or contain. Spiritual drunkenness brings man to strange and remarkable behavior. It makes some sing and praise God because they are filled with joy. It makes others weep fat tears of pure heartfelt pleasure. Still others it makes restless in all their limbs, so that they have to run, jump, and dance. This drunkenness overwhelms others to such an extent that they begin to clap their hands and applaud. One shouts in a loud voice to show the fullness he feels inside. Another has to melt away in silence because of the bliss in all his senses. Sometimes it seems to him that the whole world feels what he experiences. At other times it seems to him that nobody has ever tasted anything like this before. It often appears to him that he never can or shall lose this bliss. Sometimes he is amazed that not all men become religious or divine, but at other times it seems to him that God is his alone and that he does not give as much to anyone else as he gives to him. And yet he asks himself in amazement what this blissfulness is, or whence it comes, or what has happened to him.

On the level of physical experience this is the most blessed experience man can receive on earth. Sometimes this feeling of blessedness becomes so intense that man is afraid his heart will give out under the influence of God's gifts and their consequences (CC-CM 103, pp. 326–330).

Shortly after 1213, Jacobus of Vitry wrote the biography of the beguine Maria of Nivelles. He dedicated the work to Archbishop Fulco of Toulouse. In an introductory letter to Fulco he describes the beguines of the bishopric of Liège and the phenomena he observed among some of them.

You observed certain women here whose souls were so full with emotion and love of God that they became sick with longing and could hardly get up out of their beds for years. Their illness had no other cause than the Beloved, who made their souls melt away with longing. The more power they experienced in the spirit, the weaker their bodies became. They rejoiced in their hearts, even though they were so diffident that they did not voice this joy in their words.

One of the women was given the gift of tears with such abundance that she could not think of the Beloved in her heart without tears flowing abundantly from her eyes and leaving visible traces on her cheeks. Yet these tears in no way weakened her intellect; rather, they filled her spirit with abundant light.

Other women would be transported out of themselves in ecstasy by *spiritual drunkenness* to such an extent that they were unable to speak a single word for days. For the peace of the Lord overwhelmed their senses and paralyzed them so much that no human voice was able to take them away from that ecstasy. They also did not experience the least physical pain, no matter how sharply they were pricked! I knew a woman who would regularly experience a spiritual rapture (raptus) up to twenty-five times a day. In my own presence this experience descended on her more than seven times . . . ! When she regained normal consciousness she was full of joy because she had been in the company of the Beloved, and she would say with the words of David, who danced before the ark: "My heart and body both rejoice in the Lord" (Ps 83:3).

When some of these women received the holy Eucharist they were not only strengthened in their hearts, but they also felt an extraordinarily sweet taste in their mouths, a true comfort of the senses. The holy Body of the Lamb of God not only fulfilled their inner life, but their body was also filled with a wondrous taste. Some of them were driven to this holy sacrament by a desire so strong that they found it impossible to miss the Eucharist for a long time. They did not find comfort or peace anywhere, and they seemed to completely lose their senses with longing if they did not regularly receive this sustenance of their souls. I know a holy woman whose longing for Jesus's Body was so great that the Lamb of God itself came to her so that she would not suffer this yearning any longer. He Himself reached out the holy host to her and once she had been satisfied she completely regained her health (Acta Sanctorum Iunii IV, pp. 637–638).

5

The Ideal of the Common Life

Ruusbroec sees the highest degree of spiritual life in the "common man." "Common" here means "community-minded" and the common man dearly wants to share all he is given and all he possesses with everybody else: he is interested in the general welfare of the community. The Brothers and Sisters of the Common Life understood this fundamental thought of the Groenendaal mystic very well and their communities tried to live and propagate that ideal. In the history of spirituality Ruusbroec was the first to consciously relativize the meaning of the purely contemplative life. "Mary has chosen the best part, and that shall not be taken from her" (Luke 19:42). On the basis of this word of the Lord most spiritual writers represent the contemplative life as the highest stage of the spiritual life. Ruusbroec does not agree with that appreciation. In his opinion contemplative enjoyment and carefree work should alternate in a life that is one with God, since that is the only way in which that life will run on the rhythm of Holy Trinity. A truly spiritual man therefore does not have to make a choice between Martha and Mary. He imitates both by working when the need of his fellow men demands it, and by resting at the Lord's feet when given the chance. Christ Himself left us the best example of the common life.

> The man who is sent back to the world from the nearness of God is rich in all virtues. He possesses a rich, mild foundation founded in the richness of God. That is why he has, of necessity, to share his wealth with all those who need it. This richness flows out of the living fountain of the Holy Ghost that

can never be exhausted. He is a living and willing tool of God, with which God works what He wants and how He wants. That is also why this man does not claim any merit for himself, but he gives all honor to God. In that way he possesses a common life, because contemplation and work come just as readily to him and he is perfect in both. For nobody can possess this common life unless he is a contemplative man. And nobody can contemplate and enjoy God if he does not order his life according to God's will (CC-CM 110, pp. 180–182).

Life According to the Rythm of the Triune God

The Spirit of God exhales us so that we may love and awaken to virtue. He draws us back into Him to rest and to enjoy: that is eternal life, just like we exhale the air that is in us and inhale new air, because that is what our mortal life consists of.

Even though our spirit is unspirited and its work falls away in enjoying blessedness, it is renewed afterwards in grace and love and virtue. To go into an inactive enjoying and to go out in good works and always to stay one with the Spirit of God, that is what I mean. As we open the eyes of our body, see, and then close them again, so quickly that we do not even notice, so do we die in God and live again out of God and remain one with God always . . . .

We must therefore continually go up and down the rungs of our heavenly ladder, both by means of inner prayer and by means of external good works according to God's commandments and the decrees of Holy Church. Through the likeness with God our good works give us we are united with God in His fruitful nature that is always active in the three Persons and brings all good deeds to perfection in the unity of His Spirit. There we are unspirited to ourselves and there the Father and the Son embrace us in eternal love and enjoyment. And this is a process that renews itself continually: it begins, unfolds itself, and receives God's perfection. Here we are blessed in knowing, loving, and enjoying with God (*Werken* III, pp. 269–270).

Christ is a Perfect Example of the Common Life

We want to take Christ as an example, who was, is, and remains common in all eternity. He was sent to common humanity on earth, for the benefit of all men who would turn to Him. He says he was sent only to the lost sheep of the house of Israel (Matthew 15:22), but he did not only mean the Jews by that. For all those who shall contemplate God for ever belong to the house of Israel.

Observe now how Christ was common and gave Himself to all in true loyalty. His inner prayer was addressed to His Father and concerned all who wish to be saved. Christ was common in His love, His teaching and exhortation, and His comforting full of mercy and generosity. His soul and His body, His life and His death and His service were and are meant for all in common. His sacraments and His gifts are common to all. Christ never took food or drink for His sustenance without being aware of the general interest of all men who shall ever be saved, down to the last day. Christ had nothing proper to Himself, nothing of His own, but everything was common: body and soul, mother and disciples, cloak and tunic. He ate and drank for our sake. Only His torments and His sufferings and His misery were proper to Him and His own, but the profit and the usefulness thereof are for the whole community and the glory of His merits will be eternally common to all (CC-CM 103, pp. 430–434).

6

Encountering God in Christ

The historical Jesus was the ideal "man for others," and therefore an example of the common life. But the earthly Jesus is not just a prophet among many others. Ruusbroec considers Him the only mediator between God and man. The spiritual adventure lived by every individual man is a separate chapter of the unique story of Christ. Jesus Himself summarizes in His person the sadness and the joy of the human encounter with God. Ruusbroec often stresses that the believer should contemplate Christ both in His humanity and in His divinity. He does not just say this out of respect for church doctrine. This guideline is connected with his view of the spiritual life, in which action and prayer must always go hand in hand. Jesus's earthly life is the mirror and example of the exercise of all virtues. But man must transcend the human in faith and love, beyond all works, to know and love Jesus in His divine glory.

Through Jesus the Visible Man to the Invisible Word of God

Jesus Christ, the living Son of God, did not attract anyone to Himself, for He Himself set the example and guided His disciples and all men towards His Father in heaven. But He was so handsome and so gracious and so lovely to look at for all who loved Him that they could not prevent their souls from losing themselves in his blessed appearance with desire and affection. And so it happened that they were hindered by His noble human nature, and that their spirit was filled to the brim with so many images that it could no longer rise up from there to the contemplation of His divine nature. And so He said to His apostles: "It is good for you that I go away from you. For if I do not go away from you the Comforter, the Holy Spirit will not come to you" (John 16:7). From this you may infer yourself that even the holy apostles whom God had called and chosen from all the peoples of the earth, were unable to receive the Holy Spirit as long as Christ walked with them in His mortal body, because they were impeded and assailed by images caused by sensual love for His noble humanity.

But after He had died, risen from the dead in glory and ascended above all the heavens in full dominion, then did He draw all things towards Himself (John 12:32). Then he has given His Spirit to all who are His, who deny themselves out of love for Him and live for Him, who die to sin and live for virtue, who leave the world and hold it in contempt, who give up all earthly love and follow Christ with love into His realm. Such people truly lead a heavenly life, since Christ lives in them both as God and as man. And so it happens that they have images and yet are without images. They are full of images concerning the life of our Lord, His passion, His death, and all virtues. And yet they are at the same time free and idle and empty of all these things. And that is why they are without images and inundated with divine clarity (sister Clara). And in this way they can go out and come in and always find living nourishment. When they see the image of our Lord's humanity they go out in a good way of life, in holy exercises, and in all virtues. Without any image they turn towards their own inner being, together with the Spirit of our Lord, and there they find and possess eternal clarity, unfathomable wealth, taste, and comfort, more than they can grasp or comprehend. And so they are abundantly illuminated from on high, and here on earth they keep the right way of life and in this way they find the true nature of love. For they love themselves and all things created "in God, towards God, and for God" (CC-CM 110 pp. 526–528).

Encountering Jesus as God and Man

These people resemble the man we read about in the gospel of Saint Luke, called Zacheus (Luke 19:1 ff). He wanted to see our Lord Jesus, who He was, but he could not because the crowd was too big and he so short and small of stature. Then he ran ahead of the throng of people and climbed up a tree in a spot where Jesus was due to pass. When He came there, Jesus looked at him and said: "Zacheus, climb down quickly, for I have to be a guest in your house this very day." And he received our Lord in his house with great joy and said: "Look, Lord, I shall give half of my possessions to the poor and if I have wronged someone I shall make it up to him fourfold." Then our Lord replied: "Salvation has come to this house today because this man has become a son of Abraham in Spirit." Because of his faith he climbed up the tree and he saw and recognized Jesus, whom he longed for. He obediently climbed down from the tree and humbly received Jesus, whom he recognized and loved, into his house. With outflowing generosity he gave away his possessions and atoned for his wrongdoing fourfold. And so he was justified, and because of this he is holy and blessed and Jesus stays and lives in him, here and in eternity.

Notice now how some people resemble this Zacheus. They long to see Jesus to know who He is. And all reason and natural light fall short in this: they are too small for it. That is why they run ahead of the crowd, i. e. they avoid all multiple creatures. And by means of faith and love they climb to the summit of their thought, where the spirit, unimaged and unhindered, reigns in all its freedom. There Jesus is seen, known, and loved in His divinity because there He is always present to the free, exalted spirits who have transcended themselves out of love for Him. There He is outflowing with the full flow of his grace and graciousness. But He says to all: "Climb down quickly because high freedom of spirit cannot maintain itself except in humble obedience of the soul. For you have to know and love Me as God and as man, elevated above all and humbled below all. And so you shall taste me, when I lift you up above all things and above yourselves in Me, and when you humble yourselves below all people and below yourselves with Me and because of Me, then I shall come into your house and live with you and in you, and you with Me and in Me." And as soon as these people know, taste, and experience this, they quickly climb down in great contempt of themselves and say with a humble heart: "Lord, I am not worthy, but unworthy to receive Your glorified body in the Holy Sacrament in the sinful house of my body and my soul. But, Lord, be merciful to me and take pity on my poor life and all my faults'' (*Werken* III, pp. 181–182).

Jesus is Our Myrrh Tree

The first substance Moses had to look for to prepare oil for anointing was myrrh. The myrrh tree is five cubits tall; that means it has the height of a man. Its fruit, the myrrh, is very green and it has a sweet odor, but it tastes very bitter. The inhabitants of Arabia, where that tree grows, burn its young shoots as they grow out of its trunk to make the tree grow better and to make it bear more fruit. Its fruit is the gum it secretes, called myrrh. This myrrh flows out of the tree through the power and heat of the sun or when the bark of the tree is injured.

We consider this myrrh tree a symbol for Jesus Christ, who was injured in His flesh. He Himself says: ''A good tree produces good fruit'' (Matthew 7:17). His abundant suffering is the good fruit we live on. This suffering is a sign of grace because it pleased His heavenly Father. It has a very sweet odor. That odor heals the sick and the wounded, resuscitates the dead, frees friends of God from hell and brings all those alive into the glory of God. But this suffering was very bitter in taste because He could only complete it with His death. Look, this suffering is a special kind of myrrh because it has flowed out of the tree through the power and heat of the sun, namely divine love. It also flowed from the tree's injuries, since our Lord's graceful body became one huge wound.

We must plant this myrrh tree, namely Jesus Christ and His suffering, in the middle of our heart. And we must burn its young shoots, namely all the thoughts His suffering calls forth in us. We have to mix those thoughts with the fire of our love, so that they awaken compassion, ardent devotion, and feelings of praise and gratitude. In this way the fruit of His suffering will always grow and increase in us.

But you must know that meditating on His suffering is very gripping and bitter for all people who love Him with great feeling. Such people are in the beginning too hasty and too indiscrete in the performance of exterior works and too hard on themselves in the mortification of the flesh. And so some of them fall into some illness; others lose the normal use of their senses, and still others get both ailments, which is even worse. That is why we have to do as the inhabitants of Arabia. They would contract serious diseases if they were to burn the young shoots of the myrrh tree as they are, because the odor is too strong already by then. So they have recourse to a ruse: they first look for the gum of another tree, called storax, and that gum they burn together with the myrrh shoots. The soft and sweet odor of the gum refreshes their inner soul and protects it against all ailments. Storax is therefore the name of both the tree and its fruit. This tree is a soft and fat plant that exudes a kind of white sap, like honey. If the sap flows down to the ground it becomes impure, but if it sticks to the tree or its branches, it turns hard and red through the heat of the sun. If it is burnt in that way the odor brings joy to all who smell it.

All of this teaches us how we have to ponder the sufferings of the Lord. We must regard His humanity as a myrrh tree, richly laden with the bitter myrrh of His suffering. And at the same time we must contemplate His divinity, richly provided with all riches and all bliss, that lets the sap of His grace flow continuously, like the storax tree. For whatever we have and are, it is all gifts, both inward and outward. They are pure and sweet as honey because they all flow from His goodness. When these gifts descend on worldly people they are contaminated. Such people do not want to serve God with their life nor with everything they received from Him. And so they make God's gifts impure. But if his gifts fall on the twigs of the tree, that is: on people lovingly united with Him, they stay pure and grow red in the heat of the sun, which is His eternal love. We must put the red gum on the fire of our own love. Then the odor becomes so sweet and so full of bliss that it brings joy to all who smell it (*Werken* II, pp. 178–180).

7

Chapters on the Eucharist

> The fruit of God is the Son of God, whom the Father brings to birth in our spirit. This fruit is so unfathomably sweet to our mouth that we are unable to swallow it or to change it into ourselves. On the contrary, it swallows us and changes us into itself (and makes us share in the divine life in that way) (CC-CM 110, p. 170).

Ruusbroec explains very succinctly the difference between material and spiritual food. What man eats and drinks materially is assimilated, digested, and used to sustain his biological life. Food and drink lose their own substance, for the most part, to become building blocks for the human body. The sacred bread of the Eucharist seems to follow the same path. But from the spiritual point of view the Eucharist works in exactly the opposite way. Man, who eats, is himself transformed into a member of Christ, who is sacramentally present in the spiritual food. Once more Ruusbroec's attention is primarily directed to the divine activity in the Eucharistic encounter. Christ hungers more for us than we for Him. If man really longs for God he does not only look for the external sign of the sacrament, but even more for the inner spiritual bond. He wants to receive God both sacramentally and spiritually.

How Christ Hungers For Us

Christ's love is demanding and mild at the same time. Even though He gives us all He has and all He is, He also takes back

> all we have and all we are. And he demands more of us than we are able to offer. His hunger is exceptionally great. He consumes us utterly because He is a greedy guest and He has a ravenous hunger. He consumes the marrow from our bones. And yet we grant it to Him willingly! And the more willingly we grant it to Him, the more taste He finds in us! No matter how much He feeds on us, he cannot be satisfied, because He has a ravenous hunger, as I said, and that hunger is terribly great. And even though we are poor He does not care, since He does not want to leave us anything, anyway.
>
> He begins to prepare His food, that is: He burns all our sins and faults in love. And after we have been purified and roasted in love, He opens His mouth wide like a vulture that wants to devour everything. For He wants to transform our sinful life and consume it in His life, which is full of the grace and glory He always holds ready for us if we want to renounce ourselves and turn away from sin. If we could see through the passionate desire that inspired Christ for our blessedness, we would not be able to restrain ourselves and we would jump into His throat. Although my words sound strange, even offensive, those who love understand me well (*Werken,* III, p. 159).

This text is not only remarkable because it describes the Eucharist as an expression of Christ's love for man—Christ longed to prepare this meal for His disciples from all eternity—but also because it contains a very remarkable image of God that can only be understood on the basis of the concise assertion: "God is love" (1 John 4:8).

The human spirit must consider God, of necessity, an omnipotent and perfect Being that possesses all happiness in Its own perfection. And yet Ruusbroec says Christ hungers eternally for our human poverty. Philosophy's perfect supreme being is hard to reconcile with the love-seeking God of the gospel.

What is the difference between these two conceptions of God? The God of the philosophers lives in the seclusion of the heavenly Olympus because he does not need anybody for His own happiness and blessedness. In fact, all earthly commerce would bring with it a threat to his self-satisfied perfection, and a limitation of it. Indeed, every relationship brings uncertainty in its wake and makes both partners vulnerable and dependent on each other. How could the Word that has become flesh take up such a helpless position in a hostile world? Jesus's words and deeds led John the Evangelist and Ruusbroec to approach the divine mystery differently. The three Persons in the godhead yearn, full of desire for each other's love and loyal abandon. They are vulnerable in and by Their mutual love. In the same way Jesus is the fanatical, yet helpless Lover, who wants to share Himself with all creatures according to every man's desire and receptivity. "He consumes us utterly, He consumes the marrow from our bones."

The sober philosopher thinks of this description of the loving God as strange and offensive. Yearning and helpless longing seem to him a sign of poverty and impotence. In the Christian concept of God they are expressions of space, openness, and receptivity. Only souls who love, understand this well because love transcends all self-satisfied possession.

How Man Hungers for God

Whoever has experienced anything of God feels an eternal hunger that is never satisfied. The power of love strives and yearns inwardly, and the created spirit strives after an uncreated good. And since the spirit desires to enjoy and it is compelled and invited by God to do so, it seeks the enjoyment of God's nearness with all its power.

Look, here begins an eternal yearning and striving after what one never totally reaches. Those who experience this are the poorest people alive, for they are voracious and gluttonous, and they have a ravenous hunger. No matter what they eat or drink, they are never satisfied, because this hunger is eternal. A created vessel cannot contain an uncreated good. That is why hunger keeps torturing eternally: God utterly overflows the human inability to reach Him.

Here, in truth, is abundance of food and drink which no one knows except he who tastes it. But full satiety in enjoyment, that is the dish that is missing. That is why the hunger is always renewed. Nevertheless in this touch of God flow honeystreams full of all bliss. And this blessedness caresses man's palate whenever the spirit can remember and observe it. But all of this happens in a created manner and below God, and because of this an eternal hunger and lack of satisfaction remain.

If God were to give to this man all the gifts all the saints possess and all He is able to give, Himself excluded, the gaping voracity of the spirit would remain hungry and unappeased. It is God's inner moving and touching that makes us hungry and makes us crave. The Spirit of God spurs our spirit; the oftener He touches us, the stronger the hunger and the craving (CC-CM 103, pp. 460–462).

To Receive Christ as Mary Received Him

If you want to receive the body of our Lord in the Holy Sacrament in a dignified manner you have to cultivate the four virtues Mary, the Mother of God, possessed when she received our Lord. The first is purity, the second true knowledge of God, the third humility, and the fourth deep yearning for God. Meditate now on the first of those four virtues, which is purity, in Mary who is your mirror. From the first moment of her conception she was pure of all faults and of all inclination towards sin. That is why God's messenger, the angel Gabriel, spoke these words to her: "God greets you, full of grace, the Lord is with you" Luke 1:28). All that is full of grace is pure and all that is pure is full of grace. So, if you want to be full of grace and receive our Lord you must be pure as Mary was.

Then meditate on the second virtue that nobody can possess if he is not pure of conscience, which is true knowledge of God. Mary possessed it in the highest possible degree after her Son, who is the Wisdom of God itself, above all people who ever existed. Yet when the angel brought the message to Mary she was startled and asked herself what that greeting might mean. Then the angel said: "Fear not, Mary, for you have found mercy before the Lord. You shall conceive a Son and bring Him into the world and you shall give Him the name of Jesus. He shall be great and He shall be called the Son of the Most High, and the Lord (that is the heavenly Father) shall give him the throne of David (that is the power of David) and He shall rule the house of Jacob in eternity, and there shall be no end to his dominion." Then Mary said to the angel: "How shall that be, since I know no man?" (That is: "I shall remain pure"). To this the angel replied: "The Holy Spirit shall come over you and the power of the Most High shall cast its shadow over you and therefore the Holy that will be born of you shall be called Son of God. And look Elizabeth, your cousin, has conceived a son in her great age and this is the sixth month for her who was called barren, because nothing is impossible for God" (Luke 1:27 ff.). When Mary heard these words and understood them well, she was taught by the angel, but much more so by the Holy Spirit. Then she said: "Behold the handmaiden of the Lord." At the very same moment when God lifted her up to the highest, she put herself in the very lowest place. The Wisdom of God taught her so. For highness cannot maintain itself except in humility, as the fall of the angels from heaven proves clearly. For what is higher than the Son of God and what is lower than the Servant of God and of the whole world? And such a servant was Christ. And what is higher than the Mother of God and what is lower than the handmaiden of God and of the whole world? And such a handmaiden was Mary. She also gave over her will in the freedom of God with great longing and spoke further to the angel: "Let it be done to me according to your word" (*ibid*). When the Holy Spirit heard this, it pleased the Love of God so well that It sent Christ into Mary's womb, He who delivered us from all evil.

Behold how we learned from Mary and from the angel; how we received God's Son in our nature through His incarnation (*Werken* III, pp. 149–152).

8

Ruusbroec as an Exegete of Holy Scripture

Ruusbroec definitely did not read and explain the Scriptures according to the method of modern exegesis, which concentrates its attention on the historical and literal meaning of the texts that have been handed down. The mystic does not hold this original meaning in contempt, but he considers Scripture mainly a message from the Holy Spirit to whoever hears or reads the sacred text. "The letter kills, but the Spirit brings to life" (2 Cor 3:6). The whole of the Bible propagates the mystery of the Word become man, and this incarnation of Christ is primarily realized by means of His inward coming into the soul of man. That is why one only understands God's words in full truth if one leads one's life according to their teaching and if one tries to fathom their spiritual sense in this way. Ruusbroec sharply opposed scholars who study Scripture to know, rather than to live by.

> There are people who are very proud of their knowledge of Holy Scripture and want to play the teacher everywhere. And those who follow them can never reach the real truth, as little as those teachers themselves. A man like that turns his eyes away from the simple light of truth that is inside him and he turns towards the many problems of Scripture. And so he remains unilluminated by God because he does not want to give up his own opinion for anybody, not even for the Spirit of God. He always wants to follow the letter and teach all things as he sees them and as they please him. This leads to much quarreling and argument, it causes unrest in the heart and represents a big ob-

stacle to true charity, because the teacher becomes angry when contradicted and arrogant when not (CC-CM 110, pp. 258–260).

A sharp-witted scholar is able to explain Holy Scripture clearly and plainly because of his abundant knowledge of the text, his sharp intelligence, and his long stay in school, even though he lives outside the grace of God. But the sweetness and the fruit that lie hidden in it he cannot taste without divine love. That is why this realm of Scripture is shown to those who love, that they may live in accordance with Holy Scripture and taste its sweetness and fruit in time and eternity. For virtue, inner consolation, and hope of eternal life: these are the Kingdom of God that lies hidden in Scripture and is revealed to those who love. But strangers cannot taste it without the grace of God, no matter what their knowledge or skill (*Werken,* I, pp. 96–97).

The following texts are examples of a moral and spiritual explanation of the Scriptures. They fit in completely with medieval exegesis. They also give us some insight in the way in which Ruusbroec preached the Word of God as a parish priest.

The Encounter with Zacheus

(Freely adapted from Luke 19:1-10)

The man who applies himself to perfection and who offers all his life and all his works to God's praise and honor and is intent on God and loves Him above all, often feels the desire to see and to know Christ his Bridegroom as He is in Himself.

When man experiences this desire, he has to do what Zacheus the publican did, who desired to see Jesus and to know who He was. He should run ahead of the whole crowd, that is: free himself from the multiplicity of creatures because those make us small and short, so that we cannot see God. He shall climb the tree of faith, that grows from top to bottom, because its roots are in the godhead. That tree has twelve branches, and those are the twelve articles of the creed. The lowest branches speak of God's humanity and of points concerning our blessedness in soul and body. The top of that tree speaks of the godhead, the threeness of Persons and the oneness of God's nature. It is to this oneness that man should hold fast on the top of the tree, for it is there that Christ has to pass with all His gifts.

Jesus passes by here indeed and sees that man and addresses him in the light of the faith: telling him that He is in His godhead, unfathomable, deep as the abyss, and surpassing all created light and all limited concepts. This is the highest knowledge man can have of God in the active life: that he reaches the conclusion, in the light of faith, that God is incomprehensible and unknowable.

In this light Christ speaks to that man's longing: "Climb down quickly, because I must be a guest in your house today" (Luke 19:5). This climbing down quickly is nothing but immersion with desire and love in the abyss of the Godhead which no intellect can reach by means of its created light. But where the intellect remains outside, desire and love go in. Where the soul inclines itself towards the Lord full of yearning and with pure intention, beyond all its intellect can grasp, that soul lives and rests in God and God in it. Where the soul climbs with yearning above the multiplicity of creatures, above the activity of the senses, and above the natural light of the intellect, there it meets Christ in the light of faith, it is clearly illuminated, and understands that God is unknowable and incomprehensible. Where it inclines itself with desire towards the incomprehensible God, it meets Christ and is filled with His gifts. Where it loves and rests beyond all gifts, beyond itself, and beyond all creatures, it dwells in God and God in it (CC-CM 103 pp. 272–278).

The Centurion

(Freely adapted from Matthew 8:5-13)

Some people are much like the centurion, who was a believer in spirit, but pagan and uncircumcised in his nature. He had a hundred armed men under him, who always served and obeyed him. But he had a servant who lay ill in bed at home and was terribly ravaged by gout. He prayed to our Lord for him, that He might heal him. And our Lord answered: "I shall come and heal him." Then the centurion said: "Lord, I am not worthy that You come under my roof, but speak only one word and my servant will be healed." Then our Lord praised the man's faith, and his servant was healed at the same moment.

And so it happens to these men also. As long as they feel unchaste inclinations in their nature, and a desire for sin, their affection and love for the humanity of our Lord is hindered as by a screen. Such a man is the servant of his physical nature, which is opposed to God and the Spirit and he is greatly harassed by the devil, because that physical nature refuses to follow the Spirit in the service of our Lord with affection and love. Look, these people do not have an ardent desire for Holy Sacrament as long as they have to fight in this manner. But they say with a humble heart: "Lord, I am impure and unworthy of receiving Your Holy Body in the Sacrament under the roof of my impure body. Lord, I am also unworthy of receiving all the honor, the joy, and the consolation good people enjoy in You. And so I must always recognize my poverty in tears and keep walking before Your countenance with a firm faith. Although I am poor and abandoned I shall not let go of You. I shall shout and pray without stopping until the time when Your grace and my faith heal my servant. Then I shall love You and serve You with soul and body, with my whole person and with all my powers."

Look, these people please God even more than the tender and sensitive people. For even though they are ill and tempted in their nature, without consolation and sweetness on the part of God, yet they are full of faith, devotion, and divine love in their spirit. They often have to fight the devil, the world, and their own flesh. That is why they need strong nourishment for their mind, that will allow them to overcome everything: and that is the Body of our Lord in the Holy Sacrament. They will always receive Him if such is in accordance with the regulations of their order, if they have to say Mass, or if the good behavior of other spiritual people allows them to do so (*Werken* III, pp. 178–180).

Poor Lazarus and the Rich Miser

(Freely adapted from Luke 16:19-31)

Meditate on the judgment Christ rendered on the rich miser who wore fine purple garments, who was able to eat and drink in luxury and pleasure every day, but who never shared anything with anybody. When he died he was buried in hell by the devil. He is tortured and burns in the fire of hell and he wants a drop of water to cool his tongue, but no drop can reach him. Poor Lazarus, who lay before his door, hungry and thirsty and full

of boils, wanted the crumbs and the pieces that fell off the table, but they would not give them to him. But when he died
angels into Abraham's bosom him bore
where great joy without sadness he wore,
a life eternal without need any more (*Werken* III, p. 230).

The Coming of the Holy Spirit

And because they had seen with their own eyes how Jesus had ascended to heaven, the disciples were unable to think of anything else any more. Yes, they followed Him with unquenchable desire, with taste deeply felt, and with ardent love. They abandoned themselves to fasting, watching, and praying. The whole time they longed in all humility for the Comforter Jesus had promised them. And ten days later—the fiftieth day after His resurrection—they were all together in Jerusalem, on Mount Zion, in the house where they had eaten the Pascal Lamb with our Lord, in the house where He had given them His flesh and blood as food and drink. They had now become used to meeting there. When they were all together a fierce rushing sound came from heaven, as of a strong wind. It filled the whole house they were sitting in. Forked tongues then appeared to them, like fire. And the fire rested on each of them and they were all filled with the Holy Spirit, that is, the love of God. That love drew the Father and the Son with it; and so they received Holy Trinity.

That is what we infer from the three signs God showed them there.

1. "They heard a fierce rushing of wind" and they were filled with the Father's omnipotence that freed them of fear and trepidation. And so it came to pass that they did not stand back for anyone and that they were able to do everything.

2. "They saw forked tongues on all of them." From this we understand the wisdom of the Son. By receiving it they understood all truth, taught and cultivated all virtues, and spoke all languages, no matter what country they came to.

3. Furthermore "the fire they saw resting on every one's head" teaches us that they had been so overwhelmed by God's love that this fire could never be extinguished again, neither in time nor in eternity. You must know that Christ gave His Spirit three times to his apostles, and in three ways:

1. He gave them the Spirit before He died, to work miracles with it, such as healing the sick, driving out devils, bringing back the dead. These were physical works because they then still loved our Lord with a sensible love for His humanity.

2. He gave them His Spirit one more time when He had risen from the dead, to work spiritual works with it, such as baptizing, forgiving sins, and teaching the truth. For then their spiritual love surpassed their sensible love.

3. He gave them His Spirit a third time after he had gone to heaven. That happened so they could do divine works with it and be one with God. They then possessed God in love and they were possessed by Him in the same love.

Because their love then became threefold:

1. They loved God with all their heart, sensible and giving care to all mankind.

2. They loved him with all their soul and with all their faculties, spiritual and rational.

3. And they loved Him in the deepest depths of their spirit, divinely, escaping from themselves in divine unity. Through this they received the Holy Spirit in such an abundant manner that they passed Him on to other people. For they became so rich in God, then, that Saint Peter alone converted a thousand people to the faith that day (*Werken* II, pp. 194–195).

The Symbol of the Sparkling Stone

The Spirit of Our Lord speaks about it in the book of the Revelation of Saint John: "To the victor"—that is he who transcends himself victorious in all things—"I shall give a hidden heavenly bread"—that is, hidden inner taste and heavenly joy—"and I shall give him a small sparkling stone and engraved in that small stone a new name nobody knows, except he who receives it" (Rev 2:17). This small stone is called a pebble because it is so small, because you step or tread on it with your feet without it hurting you. This small precious stone is sparkling brightly and it is red like a fiery flame and it is small and round, smooth all over and very light.

That sparkling stone is a symbol for our Lord Jesus Christ. For according to His divinity He is a ray of the eternal Light (Wis 7:26) and a reflection of the glory of God and a mirror without stain (Heb 1:3) in which all things live. Whoever conquers and transcends all things, to him that sparkling stone is given and in it he receives light, truth, and life. That stone resembles a fiery flame because the fiery love of the eternal Word has filled the whole earth with love and in love wants to burn all loving spirits to nothingness.

Moreover this stone is so small that you hardly feel it even if you tread it unterfoot, and that is why it is called "calculus," which means pebble. And this is what Saint Paul means when he writes that the Son of God "humbled Himself and made Himself small and took the shape of a slave and was obedient unto the death on the cross" (Phil 2:7-8). And He Himself speaks through the mouth of the prophet: "I am a worm and not a man, the scorn of men and an outcast of the people" (Ps 22:7). When He appeared in time he made Himself so small that the Jews trod Him underfoot and did not feel it, for if they had recognized Him as the Son of God they would never have dared to crucify Him (cf. 1 Cor 2:8). And even today He is small and held in small esteem in the hearts of those who do not love Him.

This small noble stone I speak of is completely round and evenly smooth all over. Its roundness teaches us that divine truth has neither beginning nor end, and its evenness all over teaches us that He shall weigh all things evenly, that is, that He will give to each according to his merit and that gift shall be his for ever. The last feature of the stone I want to speak of is that it is very light, because the eternal Word of the Father has no weight, and yet it carries heaven and earth in Its power. It is also equally close to all things, and yet nobody can overtake It for it transcends all creatures and exists before all and It will reveal Itself only to those It chooses to and where It chooses. And in Its lightness our heavy humanity has transcended all the heavens and it sits crowned at the right hand of the Father.

That is the noble sparkling stone that is given to contemplative man. And in that stone a new name is engraved that nobody knows, except he who receives it. For this you must know, that all spirits receive a name when they return to God. Everybody receives his own name according to the nobility of his service and the high nature of his love, and that name is therefore different from the first name of innocence we received in baptism and that is adorned with the merits of Christ our Lord. We may lose this name of innocence through sin, but if we want to follow God again, especially in the works He wants to perform in us, we are baptized again in the Holy Spirit and we receive a new name that stays with us for ever (CC-CM 110, pp. 114–118).

9

The Mystic's Symbolic Language

It is remarkable that the Brabant mystic emphasizes the importance of image-less prayer while at the same time speaking about man who seeks and worships God in a language so rich in images. Symbolism is an important part of Ruusbroec's use of language. In this he is a typical representative of the late Middle Ages. His contemporaries read with rapture the symbolic representation of the most spiritual insights and experiences. This yearning for the symbolic has been masterfully described by Johan Huizinga in his book *The Waning of the Middle Ages.*

> The ethical and aesthetic value of the symbolical interpretation of the world was inestimable. Embracing all nature and all history, symbolism gave a conception of the world, of a still more rigorous unity than that which modern science can offer. Symbolism's image of the world is distinguished by impeccable order, architectonic structure, hierarchic subordination. For each symbolic connexion implies a difference of rank or sanctity: two things of equal value are hardly capable of a symbolic relationship with each other, unless they are both connected with some third thing of a higher order.
>
> Symbolist thought permits of an infinity of relations between things. Each thing may denote a number of distinct ideas by its different special qualities, and a quality may also have several symbolic meanings. The highest conceptions have symbols by the thousand. Nothing is too humble to represent and to glorify the sublime. The walnut signifies Christ; the sweet kernel is His divine nature, the green and pulpy outer peel is His humanity,

> the wooden shell between is the cross. Thus all things raise the thoughts to the eternal; being thought of as symbols of the highest, in a constant gradation, they are all transfused by the glory of divine majesty. Every precious stone, besides its natural splendour, sparkles with the brilliance of its symbolic values. The assimilation of roses and virginity is much more than a poetic comparison, for it reveals their common essence. As each notion arises in the mind the logic of symbolism creates a harmony of ideas. The special quality of each of them is lost in this ideal harmony and the rigour of rational conception is tempered by the presentment of some mystic unity (Pelican A307, London, 1955, p. 207).

Ruusbroec's symbolic masterpiece is undoubtedly his long treatise *of the Spiritual Tabernacle.* In it he interpretes the symbolic meaning of the ark of the covenant and of the liturgy in the Jewish temple. The golden seven-armed candle-holder is given a commentary of twenty-five pages of printed text. What a feast for the medieval reader! The following shorter texts offer a few examples of symbolic descriptions to the modern (and therefore hurried) reader.

Be Like the Eagle

> The eagle has little flesh, but many feathers. In the same way those who love God and intend to seek Him do not care much about flesh and blood and all that perishes. But they have many feathers, that is, exercises which are light and lift them up to God. And just as the eagle flies above all other birds, so also love and intention fly above all other virtues towards Him who is loved and intended. The eagle also has a sharp, penetrating eye, and with it he stares unblinkingly into the light of the sun. The person who seeks and loves God does likewise: he contemplates the rays of the eternal sun without flinching. He loves at the same time God Himself and all virtues that adorn man and lead to God. In that way he is just and flies to where he loves and always back down again where he exercises himself in virtues and good works. In this way he comes and goes like lightning in heaven. Ascending and descending is his life and his nourishment. And so does the eagle. From the highest point of his flight he still spots the little fish in the sea, the food by

which he lives. And so he flies up and down and both movements assure him of his food (CC-CM 102, pp. 180–182).

The Bee's Example

I want to introduce a small example here so that you do not go astray, but may govern yourself well in this state. You should pay attention and do as the wise bee. It dwells in unity with the community gathered around it. It does not fly out in times of storm, but when the weather is calm and still, and the sun shines, to all flowers in which sweetness can be found. It does not linger on any flower, nor with any sweetness or beauty, but it sucks honey or wax from them, that is, sweetness and matter for illumination. Then it brings that into the unity of the communal beehive so that it may bear fruit to the greater benefit of all.

When Christ, the eternal sun, shines into the open heart, He makes the heart and all the inner faculties grow and flourish and flow with joy and sweetness. Then the wise man should do as the bee. He shall fly with an attention and with reason and with discernment onto all the gifts and all the good God ever worked for him. And with the stimulus of love and of inner attention he shall taste the multiplicity of all consolation and goodness and yet not rest on any of the flowers of the gifts themselves, but fly back, all laden with gratitude and praise, to the unity where he shall rest and dwell with God in eternity (CC-CM 103, pp. 334–336).

The Water Lily

We must adorn the purple curtains of the tabernacle (that is our generosity) with the water lily. It is a symbol of the free possession of all God's rich treasures. When we look at the water lily we see four things. It always floats on the surface of the water and four green leaves stand between the flower and the water. It is well-anchored in the ground with its roots. Its crown stands open to the sun above. It is a medicine for all people who are hot with fever. In our generosity and freedom of spirit we possess all God's overflowing riches. And we have to put four green leaves between our spirit and the floodwaves of God's mild gifts. This means: we have to observe lovingly how God's eternal generosity makes always new gifts bubble up; how those gifts flow out in different ways, depending on how the loving souls receive them; how the first and most important origin of those gifts is to be found in the generous soil of divine love; how the second and near origin of those gifts is to be found in the wise and generous soil of creatures developing their resemblance to God. For nobody can know or possess the wealth of God's gifts, except a wise and generous man who is able to share God's rich abundance with all his fellow men in a wise and generous manner. In this way we have to adorn the curtain of our generosity.

In this way we shall find a solid foundation in the ground of all gifts, which is the Holy Spirit, like the water lily that is rooted in the soil under the water. And above all we must keep our heart open to the truth and the sun of justice. And in that way we become a medicine for all people. For a generous heart that possesses God's wealth can but give, console, and refresh, and bring God's shelter to all who suffer from sadness (*Werken* II, p. 50).

The Sunflower

We must adorn the white curtains of the tabernacle with yellow-gold sunflowers. These are a symbol of obedience. For when the sun rises in the East the sunflower stands open for the rays of the sun and it turns along with it to the West and turns itself towards the warmth of the sun's rays. But at night it closes itself, hides its colors, and waits for the new sunrise.

In the same way we have to open our heart in obedience to the shining in of God's grace and we must humbly keep following God's grace as long as we feel the heat of love in us. And when the light of grace no longer touches us, if we do not feel the heat of love much, or not at all (that is the night of the soul), we must close off our heart for all that can tempt us. In this way we shall hide golden colored love in our heart and look full of expectation for a new sunrise that shall touch us again with new light (*Werken* II, p. 49).

The Golden Penny

Let everyone test and examine his penny to see whether it is of fine gold, of the correct weight and well-coined on both sides.

Understand this now. If we love God for Himself and for no other motive our penny is of fine gold. And if we love, use and employ all other things for God, so that God's love has the upper hand in everything, our penny is of good and sufficient weight. And if we follow Christ, bear our cross, subdue and kill our nature in resistance (to temptation) and penance, and if we are also obedient to our superiors, to the law and the commandments, to our reason and the life of our Lord Jesus Christ, then Christ lives in us, and we in Him. And that is how our penny is adorned, formed, and well-coined on the head and we must adorn it ever more with virtues, in imitation of the life of Christ. The blank side of our penny is the essence of our soul, in which God has printed His image. And if we turn inward through faith, hope, and love, and so love and possess God, we receive His image supernaturally on the blank side of our penny. For the blank side of our penny, which is our inward-directed life, is shaped and adorned with the image of Holy Trinity, namely God Himself, because there God lives, and we in Him. And so the blank side of our penny is adorned with the indwelling of God and the head with our virtues and the life and the merits of our Lord Jesus Christ. And this is the golden penny that is worth eternal life, for it is itself eternal life (CC-CM 102, pp. 124–126).

The Illuminated Air and the Glowing Iron

If through active love a man wishes to penetrate the love that enjoys God, all the powers of his soul must retreat and suffer and endure the piercing truth and goodness that is God Himself to come over him. For, in the same way that the air is bathed with the sun's light and heat, and just as iron is penetrated by fire so that with the fire it does fire's work for it burns and lights like fire. And I say the same about the air, for if the air could reason it would say: "I give light and I give warmth to all the world." And yet they each keep their own nature, for the fire does not become iron, nor the iron fire, but their union is without intermediary, because the iron is in the fire and the fire in the iron. And so, too, is the air in the light of the sun and the light of the sun in the air.

In the same way God is always in the essence of the soul. And when the higher faculties turn inward with active love they are united with God without intermediary, in a simple knowledge of all truth and in an essential feeling and tasting of all good (CC-CM 101, pp. 128–130).

The Four Evangelists and Their Symbols

The four legs of the table in the ark are a symbol for us of the four gospels in which all prescriptions have found their perfection and on which all our works of love are founded. That is why all our works of love must join themselves to, and be in accordance with the one law of the gospels. That law has four faces, or is represented by means of four symbols, as Saint John described them (Rev 4:7), and also the prophet Ezekiel (1:6).

By means of the first symbol, love teaches us that we must overcome in ourselves all that is not in accordance with God's will and that we must subdue our animal inclinations. We then receive a spiritual life and we receive the appearance of a *lion* that subdues all wild animals and rules over them.

By means of the second symbol, love teaches us to offer ourselves and all our works to God for His eternal honor. In this way our inner life receives the appearance of a *calf,* because the calf is the symbol of the sacrifice that is offered to God.

By means of the third symbol, love teaches us true justice and leads us to a rational life, adorned with virtues. In this way our inner life receives the appearance of a *man* and at the same time it receives dominion over the whole world.

The fourth symbol testifies that love lifts some people above their own faculties to a vision without images and widens their spirit endlessly or makes it receptive to imageless spaces. There these people feel that their inner eyes are always open and without any difficulty they see the manifest revelation of eternal truth. Through this experience their love and desire grow and they long continuously to comprehend the incomprehensible God. In this state man receives the appearance of an *eagle* and a secret knowledge of God and a clear insight into the virtues, the spiritual exercises, and all the truth he needs (*Werken* II, pp. 290–291).

10

A Sober View of People and Situations

To most people, the attention to mysticism seems a useless occupation, estranged from the world. You cannot make a living out of it. Moreover, the question remains whether the mystical experiences make the seer and his environment better and happier. It is impossible to overcome all misunderstandings about and prejudices against mysticism at once. Ruusbroec's life and teaching at least refute one current opinion, namely that mystical experiences obstruct the view of sober everyday truth. The heavenly light did not blind his eyes to very earthly facts and situations. In a letter to sister Margriet van Meerbeke we read a crystal clear description of what happens in a convent without religious inspiration. Those who have entered it for the honor and glory of God begin to seek their own honor and profit. Those who lack God look for comfort and consolation in earthly things. After that there originates a faction of like-minded people who cling to each other, speak for each other and favor each other in all things to the utter detriment of mutual love in the convent.

In the book on *The Spiritual Tabernacle* Ruusbroec wrote a long and sharp accusation against abuses in all ranks of the Church. He uses such frank language in doing so that brother Geraert left out the whole offensive passage when he copied the manuscript. The mystic visionary suddenly became too concrete! These texts not only offer abundant information about the factual situation of the Church in the fourteenth century; they also prove how much the good prior suffered from the distance between ideal and reality. Yet there is nothing in Ruusbroec of a preaching moralist, nor of a reformer moved by social motivations. His accusation is not aimed at the social structures of Church and society. Even the clergy's position of political power is not condemned as such. But the whole Church apparatus seems to neglect the essential to him: to find God and to possess Him in a simple and honest soul.

Worldly Practices Behind Monastic Walls

You find many people in monasteries, in hermitages and in all forms of religious life who cannot reach such high sanctity: they are those who do not love themselves in God, towards God, or for God's sake. They look for comfort and desire solace in themselves and in the things of the earth, they seek honor and profit and they want to be raised above other people. They find pleasure in themselves and think they are worthy of all honor. All they do and leave undone, all they plan and decide could not be done better in their opinion . . . . And for this reason nobody is able to teach them anything, show them the way, or reprimand them with any chance of improvement, because they are by nature foolish and arrogant.

They want to closely observe other people, judge them and criticize them, because they do not know themselves. They are stubborn and irritable. All they do and leave undone they want to dress up in reasons and they maintain that they are right in every way. And that is why nobody can question their opinion or judgment and why there is no chance that they will listen to another. They love their own will and judgment so much that they do not obey anyone who wants anything else than they do. They are arrogant by nature and they have not yet overcome that nature in themselves. Nobody can be close to them except those who are able to flatter and pretend and who remain obedient to them in all things. To all those who do not feel for them they show a melancholy face and they spurn these opponents in word and deed. They are delicate and dainty in matters of food and drink, of clothing and all things that belong to them personally. They are happy or sad because of temporal things like other people who are still in the world. They are exceptionally worried about themselves and busy with themselves, in great fear and trepidation of all that may happen to them in time and eternity. They think they are trustworthy, but they cannot find trust or sympathy in anyone. In all adverse circumstances they are inwardly impatient and without peace. And because they did not renounce their love of self in any way, nor submit to God's will in any way, God remains strange and unknown to them.

Where two people of that kind come together in affectionate friendship, nobody will be able to separate them again. They would rather anger all other people, than do or say anything against their friend in any way. They cling so strongly to each other and they are so strongly connected that one cannot touch the one with sadness or joy without touching the other at the same time. And when such people think up a plan they cannot carry out themselves, they change their outward behavior and show a false face to pass for friends with everyone. And they attract other people to themselves in this way and form an alliance so that they be able to push their will through. And when sisters who have another opinion hear of this, they form an opposition party and so mutual charity in the convent is destroyed and chased away. For everything that seems good to one party is bad in the eyes of the other party. In this originate hatred and envy, dissension in word and deed, recriminations, arguments and insults, gossip, defiance, falsehood and discord on both sides. And so the convent turns into the devil's dominion because nobody still wants to put up with the other or tolerate her, and so the devil rules in both parties.

If someone touches a person of the opposite party by accident, even slightly, all members of that party begin to totter, because they hang together like bats who cannot see well by daylight. And these people act likewise, because they are all convinced they are right. That is why nobody wants to give in for another or tolerate another. On the contrary, they want to oppress each other and resist in all things. Those with the greatest power think to be the best. Such is the way of the world that pours poison for all men (CC-CM 110, pp. 530–534).

The Whole World Bows Down Before Worldly Goods

All animals that live under the earth, like mice and moles, were impure in the eyes of the Jews and it was forbidden to eat them. These animals are for us the symbol of rich and greedy misers. For such people are covered by worldly goods and like the moles they have good ears, but their eyes do not see at all. They come

> and attend mass, listen to the sermons, and hear the word of God, but they do not want to understand that one must spurn temporal things to obtain what is eternal. And so their vision is totally blind. What they do see is that the whole world bows down before worldly goods: popes and bishops, princes and prelates. Worldly and spiritual lords all bend the knee before worldly goods. Indeed, one is prepared to do a rich man any spiritual service he might want: one sings for him and one reads for him. All Holy Church can do outwardly is at his disposal. Without any difficulty he gets letters guaranteeing that he has been absolved of purgatory and of sins. And so he builds up reckless confidence, begins to work hard and produces great heaps of worldly goods, just like the moles are wont to do. And at the moment when he least expects it the devil comes and gets him in his warrens under the earth, that is he comes to get his soul back from his body and all his worldly goods. Then the priests begin to sing loudly and all bells begin to ring. They bury him in front of the altar and they absolve him of all the torments of purgatory. But if he died in injustice, all the living working together are unable to save him from the pains of hell. If they gave all his possessions to the poor, it would not help him one whit. Therefore everybody has to investigate his own way of life and put things in order as long as he is given the time to do so (*Werken* II, pp. 321–322).

"The whole world bows down before worldly goods": the spiritual foundations of Willem van Duivenvoorde (+ 1352).

Through his rich donations he obtains many spiritual favors. The general chapter of the Carthusians awards him, as founder of the Carthusian monastery at Geertruidenberg, the "fraternitas ordinis" in 1338. That means he is allowed to share in all of the order's prayers and good works. After his death he will be given the same prayers in all Carthusian monasteries as a deceased member of the order. On June 24, 1342, the Friars Minor of Brussels and Mechelen promise that mass will be said for him every day at Saint Clara's altar. As long as he lives special masses will be said for him on the octave of the feast of the Holy Angels and on the octave of Our Lady's Conception. After his death a solemn mass will be said for him every year on the day of his death. Two days later, on June 26, 1342, the Mechelen Augustinians award him the same favors. Their example is followed on August 6 by the Brussels Carmelites, on August 23 by the Mechelen Carmelites, and in July 1343 by the Friars Minor of Leuven.

He manages to obtain a full indulgence from the pope for the hour of his death—not once, but twice. This favor is awarded to him in a bull of May 21, 1348, and confirmed in a second bull of May 28, 1350.

This rich courtier of Jan III was in great need of these spiritual favors. He left no fewer than eight illegitimate children behind and he was fully aware of his "injustices." Not infrequently did he lend big sums of money at usurious rents of twenty to thirty percent. It is to be hoped that he did not put his trust in the letters of indulgence alone that might "absolve him from purgatory, but not from eternal hell" and that he will have helped himself, too, following Ruusbroec's wise counsel "because if they would give all his possessions to the poor, it would not help them."

A Pamphlet Against the Abuses in the Church

The Worldly Spirit Among the Laity

When a man has a new suit made it has to be pleated, with deep and pointed incisions at the neck and the arms, and with long fringes. Moreover, the suit itself is so tight and so short that he can hardly cover his shame with it. So women look at it and they make such tight clothes themselves—a shame. They line their clothes inside and outside and they invent all kinds of things to be able to please. On their heads they make mountains of hair, and those are nests in which the devils hide. Young ladies who are proud to belong to the nobility want to wear crooked horns on their heads, like goats, the better to look like the devil. And afterwards they go look at themselves in the mirror to see if they are pretty enough to please the devil and the world . . . .

These people are lazy and slow to serve God, but hasty and quick to please the devil and their own flesh. At night, when good people sleep and rest, they go dancing and feasting, eating and drinking, and indulging their lust. In the morning, when good people get up to serve God, these slaves, who served the devil, go to sleep, because they take the day for the night (John 17:12). Others do go to church and attend mass, but only to be able to show their fashionable appearance to the people. Look, they all make up that world for which Christ did not want to pray to his heavenly Father (John 17:9). And they do not desire it either because they live without any spiritual feeling and without desire for any virtue. In this way they are the young sons from the gospel, who moved away to a foreign country and lived there in lust after they had already received a part of their inheritance from God. But the eldest sons, who stayed at home with their father and possess his inheritance, those are the prelates of Holy Church and all those who live off the inheritance of our Lord Jesus Christ. It seems that they have all fallen asleep because of their great slowness, because they neither live nor teach, speak nor work to improve their people.

The Worldly Spirit among Prelates

Yet Christ entrusted these prelates with the sheep for which He Himself suffered death, but that does not touch them. Their sheep lose their way and err, but they do not care. Although their sheep are sick and wounded, they do not anoint them. Although they are injured and crippled, they do not bind up their wounds. Although the devil and the world drag them along into the abyss of hell, they do not show them the way of truth. The good shepherd walks in front of his flock: he calls, he pulls, he comforts his sheep with the promise of God's grace. He also comes behind the flock, and then he reprimands, scolds, and threatens with God's justice. Those who do not act in this way look more like the wolf than like the shepherd. The good shepherd tries to gather all his sheep into the sheep's pen, but the greedy wolf bites them to death on the field (John 15).

Let us observe whether the princes of Holy Church are good shepherds. Their salons and palaces are full of people who serve them. You see power and riches there, and great splendor as is the manner of the world, abundant food and drink, a large choice of clothes, valuable jewels and all the pomp the world can offer. Yet they are not to be satisfied: the more they receive the greedier they remain. In this way they utterly resemble the wretched world that is always out for worldly goods, because they have no taste for God.

But Christ (the Good Shepherd) teaches us another way, because He had neither house nor hermitage. With the price of His life and all His possessions He acquired man, that is His little sheep. At the moment when the world showed Him its highest honor He was sitting on an ass. His entourage then consisted of the apostles who followed Him on foot. And yet, He would have been able to find a horse, then, or a white mule if He had wanted to! But He wanted to teach us the way of humility. Therefore, we also see that in the time of the primitive Church, the apostles and holy bishops of those days traveled all over the world on foot with great zeal and converted the people from false faith.

The Rule of Bishops and Abbots

But now we see exactly the opposite. When a bishop or an important abbot visits his people, he rides with forty horses, with a great entourage, and at enormous cost. He does not have to pay himself anyway. His visitation fleeces the purse of his subjects without touching their soul. He must be given pomp and circumstance, great feasting, and abundance of food and drink, or big buttons of gold. And when he has received those the visitation and the chapter are over, because they do not want anything else. Whoever is subject to their power, canons, monks, or monials, they all have to pay. Such must be the custom, since I know of no other explanation. The subjects pay against their will, but the bishop receives with pleasure. In this way the abuses do not grow smaller, but bigger.

The Rule of Deans in the Countryside

Deans in the countryside also regularly call together the chapter of their priests. But you can see every day how much the priests improve their way of life. Those deans have yet another habit, namely that they visit every parish once, to render justice on public and grave deadly sins. Those who are found guilty of these have to give money. Such is their penance for their sins. After that they are allowed to live on quietly in the same way and serve the devil all year until the same conciliation money is levied again. Even if they are begging for their daily bread they still have to pay the money. But if they are rich, and if they have been accused of important misdeeds, they have to give much money—indeed, the highest possible sums are demanded of them. That way they are absolved from year to year, until the moment when the devil himself comes and takes them away to the pains of hell that are without end. And so everybody gets what he wants: the devil gets the soul, the bishop the money, and the foolish people their short pleasure.

This is the income the bishops and their servants live on. And even though some bishops are holy and well-intentioned, their servants and officials are evil and ruthless and so greedy that nobody can approach them or ask a favor of them without paying them well. And the highest bidders achieve the most in these courts. Absolution, letters, seals, and bans: those who have much money receive them all. And this hateful illness is contagious: it has spread and infected the whole of religion and all the clergy of the whole world. And so the cold Winter has chased away the hot Summer. Because of this only a few spiritual fruits have remained in Holy Church.

The Clergy's Hunger for Money

You can see for yourself: even though a man has four or five *prebends* at the same time, he always wants more. And the more he has, the less he deserves them, because those high lords only want to say mass on the high holidays. Their chaplains have to stand in for them on other days. They are so taken with themselves that they think it unseemly for them to say mass, unless on holidays. Even though they are of low descent, they become arrogant the moment they begin to make a career. Although they are very learned and gifted with worldly wisdom, if they chase after earthly possessions and worldly honor they are blinded in their spirit and obtain no knowledge of any virtue. The pope may give permission for them to possess various prebends, but he cannot give them permission to be greedy and miserly. Greed and miserliness are therefore two prebends the devil gives to some rich religious people and canons and they can keep those prebends for all eternity. And in that way they are unfaithful both to God and to their own conscience, because they want big prebends that give little trouble. And if the prebends were totally free and did not oblige them to any liturgical service in honor of God, they would even prefer that. Most against their will they would then pay a poor little priest the wages of hunger to sing for them, say mass, and serve God. They make a big fortune for themselves from the possessions of the poor. With what is left in their hands they buy new dividends, or start a trade. Some spend it on beautiful and valuable clothes, on tasty food and drink. Others waste it on dice or card-games or spend it on other dishonorable things. Still others neglect mass and offices even though they are legally obliged to attend them and become managers and stewards for burghers, to manage their levies and dividends, and so they are busy with what is not their business. In this way they save on their own possessions in a miserly fashion, and gain their sustenance from others in a greedy manner. Sometimes they escort high placed ladies to church and render them humble service, although that is not fitting, either to them or to the ladies. You also find other clerics who go stand in church in an undignified manner to beg for alms as if they were crippled or blind. It is right to fear that many more masses are said for material profit than for the honor of God. You hardly find one who is content with what he has. Whoever already has a prebend is glad to add another one when given the chance.

Abuses in the Choral Prayer

You can see for yourself when they ring the bells for the service of the Lord, for matins or some other office. If there is money to be made everybody gets up in a hurry and runs to church in thick throngs. But if there is nothing to be gained the bells can be rung until they break to wake them from their deep sleep: nobody appears, except for those who have to, namely the substitutes and the religious sent for that office. Rarely does anyone come there purely and only for the honor of God. And even if the high lords appear, they contribute little to edification because they either talk among themselves, or they remain silent the whole time, or they leave again, quickly, at the slightest opportunity. They do not find the least taste in the service of God.

Abuses among Priests

You also find religious men who have to take care of the people and to whom the care of souls has been entrusted in the name of God. Neither their life nor their works are to be imitated and their words but rarely, because their words often resemble their works. And so all values are rotten in the core, alas. For sin and shame have become honorable deeds, at least in the eye of the world, but not before God's seat of justice. Religious people who live off the goods of Holy Church should be pure in soul and body. And yet there are those among them who allow their children to run around in their own house, publicly, and without shame, indeed with great satisfaction as if they had been given them by a legal spouse. If the priesthood had lived as offensively at the inception of Holy Church as it does today, the Christian faith would never have spread so far and wide. But now all ranks have strayed far from their first ideal.

Portrait of an Abbot

You can observe the same phenomenon among monks the world over. You still find monks and nuns in monasteries and convents who strictly observe the discipline of the rule, who seem pious and ardent, and who behave in an exemplary manner in every way. Some religious are really well-intentioned, simple, and holy, but such religious are not held in high esteem. Others are bad and double-hearted and act differently from what they are. These are often chosen above the first to become prelates. And then only does one get to know their real face. They consider themselves elevated high above the others, as if goods and honor had come to them as an inheritance from their ancestors. From that moment on they no longer think of holiness, but devote themselves exclusively to the running of their earthly affairs and the exercise of their authority. They entrust the prior with the care of souls and divine services because they themselves are too hard pressed for time and too busy with so many things that they can hardly attend a mass. And whoever approaches them has to bend and bow, because they have the right to the first places of honor. That is exactly why they should consider themselves the very last in humility of heart and in faithful service to their people, because they are carrying the staff that belongs to the shepherd. With its sharp point they have to prick the slow sheep and urge them on. The straight shaft in the middle means that their holy life and their example assists the sick and weak sheep on the path of virtue. With the staff's crosier they have to make the sheep turn back that wander off to the world outside, and lead them back to the solitude.

Then and Now

For so it was in the beginning of monastic life. The old fathers, abbots and monks, left their fathers and mothers, family and friends, honor and possession in the world. They went to the wilderness and sought God and a holy life by leaving society and by seeking solitude for their heart. But now it is exactly the reverse. The abbots and monks of our time turn their backs to God and their faces to the world. They leave loneliness behind and ride and run outside, to family and friends. They look for food and drink and the pleasures of the body, and those are sometimes followed by shame and public dishonor. As long as they can hide the evil they do from the eyes of the people they care little for God or a good conscience.

Abuses among Monks and Nuns

You can see for yourself! If a sister or a nun has to go outside the walls of the convent she dresses up as if she wanted to sell herself to the world and the devil, which frequently happens. For without her knowing it she gives rise to many sins and she will have to account for them before God's seat of judgment. Look, for such people the convent is a prison and the world a paradise because they do not find the slightest taste in God and in eternal blessedness.

This, too, everybody can observe. When there are forty monks in a monastery they hardly say more Masses than is necessary—namely those at which the whole convention is present. And if they ring for matins at night four or five monks appear, who have to because they have been told to. For them it is much more a matter of having to than of wanting to. All the others sleep and prefer their rest and ease. There are many meetings and chapters. That is good and useful, and yet the religious spirit diminishes day by day. If everybody prefers to judge his neighbor, rather than himself, reproach becomes unmerciful and brotherly love is lacking in humility and concord. There are those who know no displeasure with themselves and no lament for their shortcomings: when these are reprimanded they find it hard to bear.

When the prior himself, or a monk ordered by him sounds the bell for the refectory, three or four of the youngest monks will appear there, to create the semblance of a well-ordered monastery. My lord the abbot stays in his house together with his entourage. And the rest of the monastery is sick and weak and indulges in meat and all the tasty food they can find. Those who have many dividends accumulate big heaps of money or give lavish feasts. Those who have little have to be content with less, because everybody keeps what he has and does not share with others.

Even though the abbey itself possesses great riches, it will not give more to the community of monks than it has to. If that community itself is also rich, they will eat and drink all the better, without giving anything to the abbey. Everybody collects his own dividends and takes care of himself only, as if he were living in the world. And all of this happens with the prelate's permission. For if the prelate wanted to abolish those dividends or distribute them among the community, that would only be accepted with great difficulty, or not at all. In this way they live without individual possessions, at least in their words, but, for many, not in their hearts.

The Ideal of the Beggar Orders

Now tell me yourself, can this kind of behavior be squared with the rule of Saint Benedict or Saint Augustine? It seems to me it cannot, unless those straight rules are written crooked with commentaries. Neither the color (of their habit) nor their works seem to fit those rules. For they show us a life of turning inward and renouncing the world, so as to find God and to possess Him in the solitude of our spirit. The founders of the (more active) mendicant orders possessed God in the solitude of their spirit. Moved inwardly by God and the love of their neighbor, they arrived at outward apostolate among the people and filled the whole world with their holy life and their pure teaching. They held goods and honor in contempt, as well as physical pleasures and all the comforts of the world. They followed Christ in self-chosen poverty, both inwardly and outwardly. They were sober in what they wanted for themselves, just in the eyes of God, and good for all men. They did not seek anything beyond God's honor and the general well-being of the whole world.

Later Abuses

The mendicant orders have grown very large by now. There are many brothers begging for alms, but few observe the rule. For what those first brothers left behind and held in contempt is now sought and chased after by their successors. You can ascertain this yourself in many ways. They are extremely eager for earthly goods and worldly honor, and also for spiritual honor on account of virtues they hardly cultivate. They want to eat and drink well and to wear a fashionable habit. Nothing seems too expensive as far as food, drink, and dress are concerned, as long as they can get it. They build tall churches and big houses and they try to get the rich to side with them, rather than to direct those people toward God and the cultivation of virtue. They want to pass for poor and complain about their need, and at the same time possess all goods in abundance. If they get much money for the divine service, or many gifts at the gate of the monastery or at a devoted layman's, they do not regard this as their possession, but they still spend it to the last penny. Their ingenuity stretches so far that they regard everything they receive as the possession of the pope or the people who give it to them, down to the very moment when they have spent or eaten it. But if somebody wanted to demand it back, it would certainly not be at his disposal. You find rich and poor brothers among them, just like in the world. One has three or four habits, another hardly has one. They flatter the sinner who is able to give much, but torture the poor man who has little and would therefore rather receive than give.

They organize begging forays at regular intervals, both in the city and in the countryside. They preach much in words, but little in deeds. And that is why their words bear little fruit. They seek more the wool than the sheep, that is, more their own profit than the blessedness of the people. They are misers and not to be satisfied, and nothing can make them content. Wheat and seed, eggs, cheese, and money: they want everything other people have. And if there were only one monastery within a seven mile radius, they would easily devour everything that can be found in that region. Many benefactors give to them more because of what people would say and because of their own reputation than out of Christian love. But they do not think this important, as long as they get what they want. And in this way true virtue regresses, both among them and among the people. A brother who is good at begging and brings in much is held in high esteem among them.

They say many masses and sing loudly, by day and night. For they live among the people and they must therefore try to win the people over with something. But when the brothers go to the refectory, the prior, the custodian, the guardian, and the master of the refectory go to another room to indulge in tasty food there, together with other rich brothers who collect dividends from their family or from spiritual daughters. But the poor brothers have to go to the refectory where they get the usual bread pudding, two herrings, and watery beer. The rich also think that the poor get enough when they get this, too much even. The poor envy the rich because they keep back so much of what belongs to the whole community, in their opinion. And so hatred and envy originate in this way of life that is too unequal. After eating the brothers fly out of the convent like bees out of their hive—all looking for loot. Has a rich man fallen ill in town? They immediately send two brothers with the request that he should select his burial place in their church. Other brothers run here or there or go visit their spiritual daughters, which yields few useful results, but often sires shame and scandal. Yet nobody can read them their lesson because they are arrogant and do not allow themselves to be told anything by anybody. If the community wants to send them away because of their faults, they look for powerful protectors outside to help them. If they have money, they will be allowed to stay by their superiors, very much against the will of the others. If a good man lives in their community, who is turned to the inner life and fears the Lord, and who would like to observe the old rule, they will pester him and mock him. He shall have more suffering than anyone else.

From this you can see that all orders and religious communities have become unfaithful to their origins and similar to the world. Except for the religious who do not go outside their monasteries or convents: the Carthusians and all the women who live in convents under enclosure. These remain most faithful to their origins.

For the devil has strung his nets all over the world. And all who eat worms that crawl in the world lead an impure life. Those are all the people who live according to the flesh, abandoning themselves to sloth, gluttony, an impure way of life, or other great sins. They all remain captive in the devil's nets. But God shall protect His elect from these dangers, no matter what state or order they live in. For the devil's nets have wide meshes. All that is humble and pure of sins escapes them. He cannot keep it because it belongs to God. The angels come to fetch them and lead them into the bosom of Abraham. But these have to find their sustenance more in inner exercises than in outer activities (*Werken,* II, pp. 322–333).

Against Simony

Simony means trade in spiritual goods or things (sacraments, indulgences, etc.) that are sold at high prices because of the spiritual power invested in them.

Christ gave His possessions to Holy Church and left His inheritance to it. That is, outward temporal goods and all the holy sacraments, full of graciousness and grace—all that He acquired and received through His holy death. Outward goods are there for the needs of the body, to keep it alive. The sacraments full of grace are there for the needs of our soul, to make us lead a virtuous life in a spiritual manner. Christ left that whole treasure and put it into the hands of priests and prelates. He wants them to spend it all and divide it among the disciples who serve Him and who deserve it, without any talk of buying or selling. For those goods are His free possessions and He divides them out of love in total freedom. Nobody has a right to them except those who serve Him lovingly in full freedom, to His eternal honor. Every good worker, who serves and loves, is fully worth his sustenance (Matthew 10:10). But those who live in public deadly sins and serve the devil, the world, and their flesh, are not worthy of spending the patrimony Christ bought with His blessed death. For those who want to buy or sell that patrimony and live off it unjustly, it turns to venom and eternal death.

It is allowed in Holy Church for poor priests and the religious, who read and sing for the honor of God and who serve the people by distributing the sacraments, to hire out their work and service to others and to live off their work. But no one is allowed to buy or sell the grace itself and the holy power that is hidden in it. They belong exclusively to the divine power and its work, above all human intervention, no matter how holy they are or in which state they live.

We must therefore eat and drink to be able to serve God. But this service of God should not be performed for eating or drinking, or for any transitory goods, but for Himself and His eternal honor. That is the right attitude which pleases God and makes us holy and blessed. But that attitude is little known and little sought. Those who want to belong to God and serve Him may well shout full of desire: "Stay with us, Lord, for the evening is near!" (Luke 24:29). The day of grace and virtue passes unnoticed and truth has almost vanished completely. The clergy is blind to a high degree and errs outside the straight path of truth. We must not judge, slander, or spurn anyone in our heart, for we must leave judgment to God Himself. This is expressly forbidden to us in the case of our superiors, who guide us in Holy Church in the name of God. But we are allowed to condemn sin and to praise virtue, because that was the rule our Lord Jesus Christ and His saints lived by from the beginning. You can see it yourself: Christ has left the inheritance, the power and the wealth He Himself acquired through His blood and through His holy death and entrusted it to princes and priests, leaders of Holy Church and the Christian world. They are allowed to live off it and provide for their sustenance according to just order and measure, with fitting sobriety. What is left after that should lawfully be given to the poor according to reasonable judgment and distinction. Those in authority who rule God's people in Christ's name should be humble and generous, mild and just. As true servants of Christ they should give true support to all people.

Now it is very easy to see that the true servants of God and His people are those who act according to Christian law and the precepts of the gospel. Are we allowed to count those with them who possess Christ's inheritance in abundance and great estates, in bliss and physical pleasures, and who sell their seal, their wax, and their writings at such high prices that poor, innocent people can hardly acquire them? And yet those poor people have to give what they are asked for to obtain what they need or what they seek and desire. That behavior looks more like greed than like love for one's neighbor. That is what they shall be made to hear in the hour of their death, when Christ shall say to them: "Give an account of your management because you cannot remain a steward any longer" (Luke 16:2).

Christ allows evil prelates and bad priests to have themselves elected and exalted, and to buy a prelateship and acquire spiritual dominion over His people. They spurn Christ, His life, His teaching, and His commandments. They dominate and rule God's people, not as shepherds, but as tyrants. They are cunning and jealous, greedy and miserly. They do not feed poor souls or give them to eat; not with their life, nor with words, nor deeds, nor good examples. Nor do they care for the bodies of the poor with the worldly goods they possess and keep to themselves unjustly or spend lavishly on sins.

They make their relatives rich with the goods that belong to the poor. They can easily put up with all kinds of sins, as long as they can derive some earthly profit from them. The usurer is allowed to sacrifice and serve at the altar if he is able to pay good money for it. If he dies they will carry out his will and bury him in front of the altar. They would rather see pennies than penitence for sins. Every sinner is allowed to live on in adultery and in sin as long as he pays his levy every year, according to his income and his wealth. But if he wants to renounce sin and go back to the way of life of Holy Church he shall have to buy that reconciliation with money, or he shall not be able to receive it (*Werken* IV, pp. 126–128).

Conclusions

Ruusbroec did not appear in the Low Countries like a solitary meteorite in a sky without stars. Rather, he is the brightest star in a constellation of spiritual writers. He undoubtedly knew the writings of Beatrijs of Nazareth and of Hadewijch, the great beguine. He read the Latin works of Saint Bernard, of William of Saint-Thierry and also the confusing testimony *Speculum simplicium animarum* by the beguine Margaretha Porete. The influence of famous predecessors and contemporaries has only been hinted at sporadically in this study.

Ruusbroec's spiritual teaching originated in deep personal experience. But that does not mean he did not take over many insights from the widespread spirituality of the church fathers and the monastic orders. The culture of the inner life, the spiritual experience of the Eucharist, the meditation on the Word made man, the three stages of the spiritual life, the negative knowledge of God: all of these themes are common to the spiritual authors of the Middle Ages. Ruusbroec treated them in a very personal way and brought them together in an original synthesis. But he would not be counted among the most important mystical writers of European Christendom if he had not enriched mystical literature with important new insights. In a completely original way he dealt with three themes found only in the real masters of Christian mysticism, also in later times: the trinitary character of the encounter with God, the characteristics of the common man and the human values inherent to a life in union with God.

Loving man wants to encounter God in His gifts and his desire finds neither rest nor satisfaction before the Beloved Himself personally shares Himself with him. That Beloved is described in the creed as one God in three Persons. Ruusbroec's personal encounter with God takes place in a wonderful manner according to the trinitary model of the divine life. The central dogma of the christian faith becomes for him *the* fundamental scheme of his direct experience of God.

The common man is so completely given over to the will of the Beloved that he can as easily pray in contemplation (turn inward to the foundation of the soul) as lend a helping hand (turn outward to others). This common life is not the result of any moral endeavor, but a gift of God. God allows His beloved sons and daughters to rock as waves on the rhythm of the divine sea that goes out and turns inward all the time, like ebb and flow.

Ruusbroec's humanism is primarily apparent in his concept of the union with God. When God's love overflows and penetrates the soul of man, human faculties are not annihilated, but spurred on to new activity. The so-called laming of the senses can hinder man for a while in visions and strongly emotional experiences. True union with God does not lead to languishing in impotence, nor to sinking down into the unconscious. In that case God would do violence to human dignity. "When we are united with God a living knowledge thereof remains in us, together with an active love. For without our knowledge we cannot possess God and without deeds of love we cannot be united with God, nor stay united with Him. If we could be blessed without conscious knowledge, then a stone, that has no knowledge, could also find bliss. If I were lord of all the earth and I did not know it, what would I stand to gain?" (CC-CM 110, p. 154). God does not expect man to behave towards Him like a cold stone, certainly not at the moment of the most intense encounter! Ruusbroec's writings grip and inspire essentially through the enthusiasm with which he writes about God. He has enjoyed God like no other and that is why he could write so abundantly about the bliss and the wealth, the blessedness and the sweetness, the pleasure and the joy of a life united with God. He does not deal with theological questions, nor does he give any pastoral suggestions. "There are many meetings and chapters, and yet the religious spirit diminishes day by day." He shows the religious and laymen who strayed in his day the example of the holy founders of monastic orders: they sought

God in the solitude of their heart. He himself did nothing else his whole life long. He has been allowed to possess God in an exceptional manner and he keeps sharing Him with many others.

> The soul is ignited by wonder about God's wealth, and it burns all over with ardor. This fire is the Holy Spirit, burning in the oven of divine unity. This enjoying unity is the hidden treasure in the field of the soul. Whoever tastes this joy renounces himself and sells everything to possess this field (Matthew 13:44). The Holy Spirit is the treasure of God and of the souls. He is a bond of love (vinculum caritatis) and an embrace of love by which all inward spirits are penetrated and embraced in enjoying unity. He is the love that causes the loving soul to be consumed in its glow. He is the finger of God that created heaven and earth and all creatures according to their nature. To those who seek Him, He gives His supernatural gifts according to their receptivity, and He has united these blessed ones in Himself. The Holy Spirit is the wild, wide sea from which all good has flowed and in which it can be found without measure. He is the burning, clear, divine sun that adorns the realm of the soul with its seven supernatural rays, namely his seven gifts.
>
> This is the clear sun that shines and burns in the highest part of the soul and elevates the intellect in contemplation with clarity and makes it stare without failing in eternity. This is the living, groundless source, that flows from inward to outward with seven principal rivers, namely the seven gifts that make the realm of the soul fertile, in all virtues. The eminent spirits have followed this living, pulsating artery into its ground, where the source finds its origin. There they are flowed through and overflowed from clarity to clarity (2 Cor 3:18), from bliss to bliss, for there is the dew of the honey-drops of inexhaustible joy that make the soul melt and float in the bliss of divine blessedness (*Werken* I, pp. 84–86).

Quotable Sayings

1. God is a flowing and ebbing sea which flows without ceasing into all His beloved, according to everyone's need and dignity. And all who have been gifted thus in heaven and on earth He makes ebb back with all they have and are able to do (CC-CM 103, p. 418).

2. God is more inwards to us than we are to ourselves, and His inward impulse, or working, is nearer and more inner to us than our own work. And therefore God works in us from within outwards, and all the creatures from without inwards (CC-CM 103, p. 296).

3. God gives grace to work.
He gives Himself above all grace
to enjoy Him and rest in Him (CC-CM 103, p. 296).

4. God gives Himself completely to every man in particular and yet He gives himself communally to all creatures, for through Him all things exist and in Him and on Him hang heaven and earth (CC-CM 103, p. 412).

5. The nature of love consists of giving and taking, loving and being loved. Both elements are to be found in whoever loves (*Werken* III, p. 158).

6. I am yours and you are Mine.
I dwell in you and you live in Me (*Werken* IV, p. 17).

7. Love is not silent, it shouts for ever and without stopping: "Be ready to love" (*Werken* III, p. 268).

8. Holiness is a "knighthood" which one has to preserve by battle (*Werken* III, p. 134).

9. The time is short; the labor we are able to do is little; the reward is great and everlasting (CC-CM 110, p. 598).

10. When the vessel is ready, noble liquor is poured into it. There is no vessel more noble than the loving soul and no drink more beneficial than the grace of God (CC-CM 103, p. 292).

Bibliography

Since the year 1981 the Center of Spirituality in the Antwerp Uniuersity (called also Ruusbroecgenootschap) is preparing the critical edition of the "Opera omnia" of Jan van Ruusbroec. Of the planned ten volumes four are already available. These volumes contain the original texts, the Latin version of Surius (edited in Cologne 1552) and an up-to-date English version. These "Opera omnia" are assumed in the impressive series Corpus Christianorum-Continuatio mediaevalis, edited by Brepols, Turnhout (Belgium). We give now the extant titles.

CC-CM 101: Little Book of Enlightenment (Boecsken der verclaringhe) (1989).
CC-CM 102: The Seven Enclosures (Vanden seven sloten) (1989).
CC-CM 103: The Spiritual Espousals (Die geestelike brulocht) (1988).
CC-CM 110: The Sparkling Stone (Vanden blinkenden steen)
The Four Temptations (Vanden vier becoringhen)
The Christian Faith (Vanden kerstenen ghelove)
Letters (Brieven) (1991)

For the other texts the reader is referred to the complete works of Jan van Ruusbroec published in four volumes between 1944 and 1948. All quotations identified as *Werken* have been taken from this edition of the original texts. Still we have to mention another important English text-book: The Spiritual Espousals and other Works. Introduction and translation by James A. Wiseman (The Classics of Western Spirituality, New York, 1985). This book contains: The Spiritual Espousals, The Sparkling Stone, A Mirror of Eternal Blessedness, The Little Book of Clarification.

Studies

Ampe A., Jean Ruusbroec, in: Dictionnaire de Spiritualité, tome VIII (Paris, 1974), col. 659-697.

Axters St., The Spirituality of the Old Low Countries, translated by D. Attwater, London, 1954.

De Vreese W. L., Ruysbroeck, in: Bibliographie nationale de Belgique, tome XX (Bruxelles, 1910), col. 507-591.

Mommaers P., The Land Within. The Process of Possessing and Being Possessed by God According to the Mystic Jan van Ruysbroeck, Chicago, 1975.

Mommaers P. and De Paepe N., Jan van Ruusbroec. The sources, content and sequels of his mysticism. (Mediaevalia Lovaniensia XII), Louvain, 1984.

Underhill E., Ruysbroeck (The quest series), London, 1914.

Obituaire du monastère de Groenendael dans la Forêt de Soignes, publié par M. Dykmans (Académie Royale de Belgique. Commission Royale d'Histoire), Bruxelles, 1940.